ASPECTS OF ETHNICITY

ASPECTS OF ETHNICITY

Understanding Differences in Pluralistic Classroom

WILMA S. LONGSTREET
PROFESSOR OF EDUCATION
THE UNIVERSITY OF MICHIGAN—FLINT

TEACHERS COLLEGE PRESS

NEW YORK AND LONDON

Copyright © 1978 by Wilma S. Longstreet. All rights reserved.
Published by Teachers College Press, Teachers
College, Columbia University, 1234 Amsterdam
Avenue, New York, New York 10027

DESIGNED BY CONSTANCE FOGLER

Library of Congress Cataloging in Publication Data

Longstreet, Wilma S
    Aspects of ethnicity.

    1. Minorities—Education—United States. I. Title.
LC3731.L66   371.9'7   78-16631

ISBN: 0-8077-2529-3

Manufactured in the U.S.A.

Acknowledgments

This book would not have been possible without the cooperation of my graduate and undergraduate students, who gave freely of their time, effort, and sincerity so that more insight into the nature of pluralism might be achieved. Since 1968 students have helped me to clarify my ideas about ethnicity and to transform them into improved instructional practice. I cannot thank them enough.

I also wish to extend my appreciation to Professor Shirley H. Engle of Indiana University, who patiently read and commented on several drafts of this book. His insights have been of immeasurable help.

W.S.L.

Contents

Foreword

Rarely has the concept of ethnicity been expanded to the extent that this volume attempts. Sociologists, anthropologists, and curriculum theorists have all struggled with it for generations but have been unable to adequately correlate explanations or research findings to the practical applications of classroom teaching and learning. This volume is a combination of biography-social science research findings, classroom management techniques, and a language/communication analysis system. The first declaration of a definition of ethnicity appears early in the text, and from that point the expansions begin to flow. Longstreet has made a case for *heritage ethnicity* and *scholastic ethnicity* and relates these to the bureaucracy of the American school.

In the process of exploring the concept of stereotyping in Chapter II, she treats the concept more objectively than most specialists either in curriculum or social science, and in Chapter III, a rather new insight into the dynamics of verbal and nonverbal behavior is provided.

Major statements are offered throughout this volume that, upon reading, sometimes seem evident, and yet they escape us with regard to the universality of all human beings, for example, the universal capacity to learn oral language from our families or those closest to us at our youngest ages. Chapter V also clarifies the reality that the ethnocentric bias of language categorization is so pervasive that it almost becomes unrecognized. Dialects are perceived as either negative or positive, and occupational evaluations based on nonverbal cues are constantly made.

In the subsequent chapters, Longstreet reveals that nonverbal cues are powerful in their connotations (Chapter VI) and that teachers make decisions based on much of that communication. Social value patterns (Chapter VIII) are discussed in language that permits immediate application of the background principles imbedded therein. In Chapters IX and X, the case is made for intellectual modes and for conducting action research.

For practitioners who have not afforded themselves the opportunity of action research efforts toward understanding other human beings, Longstreet has elaborated on the limitations and extensions of some basic procedures without apologizing for socially significant research. Her case for informal observations becomes one of the most personalized elements of the volume.

Making considerable use of researchers associated with the same phenomena, Longstreet has compared, contrasted, rejected, accepted, and refined much of the widely used literature relating to ethnicity and relating to schooling. The relationship of basic and advanced notions about the impact of ethnicity are critically defined through the sample profiles/checklists and the charts included throughout the volume.

As a Black American who attempted interpretation of excerpts and of anecdotes as much as the empirical accuracy, I am favorably disposed with the depth of clarity provided regarding certain ethnic profiles—presented initially through individual descriptions, then addressed through group/ethnic practices designed for understanding in relation to schooling.

Perhaps the most sobering element of the entire work is found in the Epilogue–Prologue where Longstreet admits that such a study has no end—and that our attention to it is—and can only be—a beginning at this point. The humane approach of these findings and reflections, however, provide the energy for much intellectual examination and application.

James B. Boyer
Kansas State University

ASPECTS OF ETHNICITY

CHAPTER I

Introduction: Stumbling Into Ethnicity

How I came to this study of ethnicity has considerable bearing on the form it has taken, so I shall try to give a brief account of some of the more salient details. To begin, I am a native New Yorker for whom a Jewish grandmother, dead many years, remains a vivid memory. I worked my way through college taking many part-time jobs from being a waitress to selling jewelry on 34th Street. In the process, I came in contact with a diversity of ethnic groups only possible in a city such as New York. Then, by varied and sundried twists of fate and while still in my twenties, I lived in Europe, especially Italy, for an extended period of time. I earned my livelihood by capitalizing on the several languages I had learned fluently and on what was then my somewhat unconscious ability to adapt to changing human circumstances.

In particular, I worked as tour escort for several large travel companies and as a reporter, though never anywhere near the top of the heap. In both these undertakings I often needed help from people. It was, after all, no minor feat to travel around Europe with forty Americans behind you demanding their money's worth, or following some obscure story that just might make page ten of an American daily. I was forever needing to ask people for a good turn. This was especially true as a tour escort when I was often juggling the unique traits of an Italian driver, French concierge, numerous Midwestern farmers, and my own New Yorkisms. We were all people of good will and usually ended up having a pleasurable trip.

It required a lot of adapting on my part. I can, for instance, remember how I solved my hotel room problems, which would frequently arise after crossing the Rhine and entering Germany. There were usually necessary changes because two tourists sharing a double bed could no longer stand the sight of each other or some fiancé had added himself to the tour at the last minute. In France, I would smile at the concierge, roll my eyes toward heaven with a bit of a wink, talk as though I were put out but not seriously, and it would be accomplished. I would sign some paper or other and the rooms would be changed.

In Germany, sometimes not even a hundred miles eastward, it was quite another story. Why did I want to make an un- authorized change? What assurances were there that the hotel would be paid for the extra costs? And so it would go until it was sometimes necessary to call the main American office, which was never smiled upon because of the expense and time involved. After all, why was I bothering them when room mod- ifications were part of my job?

Neither the German managers nor the French concierges had anything against me or even for me—they were just doing their jobs in a way that seemed reasonable to them. What I learned was that I had to approach German managers for room changes in a very different way from the approach used in France. This I did by formally typing (usually the night before) my room change requests on the travel agency's stationery and signing the request along with my official title of "Tour Director." I would walk into the hotel, hand the clerk my typed changes, smile pleasantly, and it was done.

After a number of very rewarding years in Europe, I returned to what had never really been home—Indiana—and began stu- dying for my doctorate. Given my experiences abroad and the fact that I had myself grown up in poor, ethnically-mixed cir- cumstances, my interest in cultural differences blossomed. Then, too, I soon realized that I stood out as a New Yorker in the Midwest—there were traits I unconsciously had, despite my many years abroad, that marked me a New Yorker. So it was that I enrolled in numerous education courses dealing with the problems youngsters of different cultural heritages might encounter in American schools.

At the time I was teaching German and English at a high school in Gary, Indiana. My German classes were unique. The high school's student population was split more or less evenly between college-oriented, middle-class, mainstream youth and a potpourri of poor blacks and first-and second-generation Greek, Italian, and Puerto Rican Americans. For reasons that are still obscure to me (perhaps the guidance department had an explanation), my German classes had few college-oriented mainstreamers and were filled primarily by potential dropouts of mixed backgrounds who shared only their total disinterest in learning German. An accounting of that year and my survival could comprise a book of its own, but, though possibly interesting, would contribute relatively little to existing insights on ethnicity and its effects in a pluralistic school setting, a purpose basic to all the studies I have pursued this past decade or so.

I survived that year and even had a few very satisfying successes that were probably the fruits of my years of cultural adaptation while living abroad, but I was keenly aware that whatever I might be doing that was right, I had little general understanding of what I was doing or why it was right. Furthermore, while the college courses I was taking increased my awareness of the injustices that had been perpetrated on minorities, especially on blacks and Spanish-speaking groups, they provided very little beyond that awareness. I participated in Operation Breadbasket activities, I tutored youngsters in economically deprived areas, I read an endless flow of articles, and I listened to innumerable speeches, but when all was said and done, I gained very little knowledge about how to be a better teacher—or even a better member of a multi-cultural society.

Most of all, I wanted to know how to become more knowledgeable about the unique cultural characteristics of the groups

I was dealing with *without* becoming immeshed in a series of stereotypes; I wanted to know how to become more insightful, more sensitive—yes, more expert in my teaching after three years than I was at the beginning of my contacts with a group. The courses I was taking and the books I read all seemed to be filled with generalizations that were very difficult to relate to the specific kinds of behaviors I actually encountered in my classroom. Then too, I found it very hard to sort out individual personalities from cultural traits unique to a whole group. The generalizations that filled my formal studies seemed to ignore these difficulties altogether.

One book I had read for an assignment about Mexican-American youth typifies the problem I was having. At the time, it was one of the most up-to-date pieces I could obtain; here is an excerpt of the discussion on respect and good manners:

> Tied to the values of honor and respect is the emphasis which the home places on respectful conduct. It is a sign of *persona educada* and is stressed as behavior to be learned by all, irrespective of social class. The individual who lacks it is *bruto* or *burro*, an outmodel of which the child is often reminded. . . .
>
> It should be noted that Mexican American youths do not think of this kind of behavior as "good manners" but rather as "being respectful."[1]

The author underlined the importance of respect and manners, but nowhere did she translate this into specific kinds of behaviors that I might encounter in a classroom. From my many years of traveling abroad, I knew it could not be assumed that members of one cultural group would understand the importance and significance that members of another cultural group might attach to certain ways of behaving. We are all carriers of cultural traits typifying our group membership and distinguishing us from members of other groups. Were my students and I really understanding each other's behaviors? I vividly recall a behavior of good manners and respect engaged in by Italians that never ceased to make me feel awkward. Italians shake hands with good acquaintances every time they encounter each other, even if they meet several times a week. By the time I returned to the United States extending my hand had become a habit, and though my handshake was usually returned, it was not without a bit of confusion and feeling of oddity. I quickly unlearned the habit.

UNDERTAKING A STUDY OF ETHNICITY

As I delved more deeply into multi-cultural studies, the desire to deal with specific behaviors representative of an ethnic group's beliefs and understanding increased. So did my problems. For example, what kinds of behaviors would I study? That question does not have an easy answer. If a scientist in an experiment follows a set of established procedures that might be called "laboratory behaviors," should these be a part of my studies? If a majority of people in a nation perceive a minority group to be lazy and unwilling to work, how should that perception be dealt with? Is that part of ethnicity?

Then, too, there was always the fear of stereotyping. How could I describe the behaviors of a group without violating the rights of individuals to personalities of their own? In what way is personality affected by group membership and vice versa? I was involved with questions that go to the very core of social scientific research. When may a generalization about individuals become a defensible generalization about the group to which individuals belong? How can the subjectivity and the cultural background of the observer be overcome in observing cultural uniquenesses sometimes quite different from those perhaps unconsciously borne by the observer?

The changing qualities of cultural characteristics pose still more questions. Is a generalization made about a group in 1970 valid in 1977? Is a generalization made about a group living in Florida valid for the same ethnic group located in a different geographic area? How important are socioeconomic differences in understanding ethnic differences? Might a group react against descriptions of their members made by social researchers and change because of the descriptions? In summary, how could I, a classroom teacher, obtain defensible information about the way diverse cultural groups in my classes acted toward each other, toward me, toward their future and, of course, toward learning? And, assuming that I did succeed in garnering some insights into specific ethnic behaviors, how could I use these to improve my teaching? This book is an account of my continuing efforts to deal with these questions since I returned from Europe in 1966.

As a teacher in a public school, I typically faced classes composed of two or three distinct cultural groups. Often my own background added to the multi-ethnic character of the classroom. I found myself repeatedly making judgments and decisions that were necessary given normal classroom requirements but that were based on ignorance. This was brought home to me vividly when, on the very same day, a young Chicano boy asked me why I was always picking on him and a black youngster accused me of favoring the "Pollacks" in the class. The accusations took me by surprise for I felt that I had bent over backwards to treat all my students fairly. Instead, the black student pointed out that whenever he came in late—even a minute or two—I would make a big "to-do," and when those other kids came in late, I would just go on talking as if it were no big deal. He was right. But why was I doing that? I realized it was the way he walked in that seemed to say (to me—perhaps not to him!) "I don't care, baby, if I'm late." It irked me but, upon reflection, I truly did not know whether he intended to communicate to me the message I had surmised from the manner he entered the classroom.

Frankly, as a teacher, I believe it is my duty to make judgments of that kind and to react in some defensible way. I have, however, no right to continue to judge without any effort to get at the truth. The young Chicano boy provided an example of how even a tiny bit of information could help me in my teaching. He sat toward the back of the room and to be sure he knew I was talking to him, I would raise my voice. For reasons

that were later to become clearer to me, he interpreted this rais-
ing of my voice as "yelling" at him, which, for him, was syno-
nymous with being "picked on." Since I had no intention of
"picking on" him, I made a conscious effort to lower the tone
of my voice thereafter whenever I addressed him.

Teachers are continually making decisions based upon how
people behave without having any real knowledge of ethnic behaviors beyond those experienced in their own backgrounds.
Furthermore, they are as likely to have stereotypic perceptions
of a group as are other members of society. I was a New Yorker
and, quite naturally, I was interpreting the behaviors of young
black Midwesterners through the framework of my own background, just as the young Chicano was interpreting my behavior
through his background. I found the bases for my teaching decisions too haphazard, too subjective, to be acceptable in a public school environment.

I could not wait for the resolution of significant social scientific research questions that would doubtlessly plague any study
of ethnic behaviors I would undertake. My decisions as a teacher were being made daily and they were involving—perhaps
harming—a lot of students. I might not only be misinterpreting
my students' behaviors but be operating on the basis of inaccurate stereotypic information without fully understanding
what I was doing. I needed more objective data about how different ethnic groups might behave under typical circumstances
in the public school. I needed to deal with my own perceptions
of an ethnic group and even with behavioral incompatibilities
that might arise between myself and my students because of the
differences in our backgrounds.

THE ETHNIC PROFILE

Ethnic incompatibilities, the misinterpretations of ethnic
traits, and the persistence of unsubstantiated stereotypes (which
might even be held unconsciously) have only infrequently been
squarely faced by public institutions. Schools have been espe-

cially reticent to discuss the traits of specific ethnic groups at any level of generalization. I realize that, at least in part, such reticence reflects the history of the United States. The ideal of being accepted for what we are without the empty pride or burdensome stigma accompanying descriptions of ethnic backgrounds (e.g., Spick, Pollack, WASP, Nigger) has been staunchly upheld by Americans whether they support a melting-pot-one-America view of United States culture or a pluralistic view that would have each group preserve the uniqueness of its heritage. In a sense, the ideal has protected the individual's inalienable right to a personality of his or her own, unhampered by the stereotypes attributed to his or her ethnic group. In still another sense this ideal has supported a conception of universal humanness. If, say, Jews are labelled as being "money hungry," the implication is that other groups are not desirous of lucrative gains. Yet, comparable desires have been found throughout the world in quite different cultures. Some Jews may be money hungry while others are not; some German or Italian Catholics may be equally money hungry while others are not.

Regardless of the benefits that may accrue from public institutions refusing to acknowledge, *in public,* general descriptions of ethnic traits, it is my conviction that this very refusal has fostered the continued use of incorrect and often unjust stereotypes about ethnic groups. A stereotype is a generalization (frequently an overgeneralization) about the behavior of a group of people. Generalizing and overgeneralizing on limited information are basic characteristics of human thought. Human beings do not stop generalizing simply because they are thinking about other human beings. Stereotyping is as natural to people as thinking itself. Psychologist Daryl Bem expressed the initial innocence of the phenomenon and its relation to human thought succinctly:

> It is important to realize that the process by which most stereotypes arise is not evil or pathological. Generalizing from a limited set of experiences and treating individuals as members of a group are not only common cognitive acts but necessary ones.[2]

We are all involved in stereotyping. To hide this from ourselves or to allow public institutions to ignore the phenomenon does not eliminate stereotypes but rather allows them to exist, perhaps as inaccurate or exaggerated generalizations, unchecked by logical examination or empirical evidence.

Stereotypes can contain basic ethnic truths about a group. Writers, actors, and comedians have long intuited the validity of stereotypes. Actors do not merely take on the accents of the characters being portrayed. If the characters are Japanese, there are certain ways actors will stand or walk or use their hands that would change significantly if the characters being portrayed were New York Jews or Montana cattle ranchers. Playwrights would modify the kinds of small talk engaged in or the way anger is exhibited according to the ethnic differences of their characters. Their representations of angry Italians would differ from that of angry Englishmen, even if their personalities were quite similar. Comedians can make millions laugh by the stereotypes that they depict. In the early seventies, Flip Wilson's impersonations of a black woman named Geraldine often prompted blacks to acknowledge that they knew someone just like Geraldine. Back in the fifties, I used to watch a TV program about a Jewish mother named Molly Goldberg, and I remember thinking that I knew a couple of people just like Molly.

Of course, there is no one exactly like Molly or Geraldine. The complexity of many different kinds of phenomena influencing our human development assures each of us of uniqueness. Notwithstanding our uniqueness, we are also each the bearers of patterns of behavior that make it possible for us to be a member of our group. It is a little like language. We express ourselves uniquely, but if we are to speak English and not German or jibberish, we must also share with others in a pattern of speaking behaviors about which generalizations (or grammatical descriptions) can be made. Playwrights, comics, and the like have long used such patterns of behavior to achieve a sense of reality. Their efforts have often been inaccurate, unexamined stereotypes that contain enough truth to be considered, by audiences, as a reflection of reality.

Teachers, too, engage continuously in stereotyping, even though their institutions refuse to deal with the phenomenon publicly. Teachers' stages are usually lounges or lunchrooms and their generalizations are often helpful suggestions about students given to fellow teachers. I remember one of these suggestions very vividly because it was so insensitive in its kindness. I was running a project on teaching to the ethnically different in twelve inner-city Chicago schools. One of my student teachers and I were sitting in the lunchroom talking to an older teacher, who was very open to the project and wanted to help. The school was a junior high with a number of Puerto Rican and Chicano youngsters. The older teacher leaned toward my student, patted her hand, and said in a lowered voice, "Honey, don't let those Mexican kids touch you too much. They don't mean any harm—they're really a good bunch—but they get too familiar."

I refrained from asking what was wrong with twelve- and thirteen-year-olds "getting familiar" if they meant no harm. Perhaps my student, because of her interest in understanding the different ways ethnic groups interact, would seek to understand the messages these youngsters intended to transmit with their touching. Indeed, she might even check out whether the older teacher's stereotypic comment about touching was actually true. But how many student teachers or first-year novices could ignore the backroom stereotype passed from mouth to mouth in professional kindness? I suspect not many.

Through the mindless efforts of public schools not to stereotype, two very serious situations have developed: *1)* the ethnic backgrounds of *all* students have been ignored, while a purported "equal treatment" based on objectively measured intellectual performance has held sway over the destinies of millions of youngsters; and *2)* the natural human proclivity to stereotype has taken refuge in backroom, off-the-cuff, though highly influential talk. The first of these problems has come to be more widely recognized as minority groups assert the right to retain and communicate their ethnic heritage to their young, and demand that schools acknowledge ethnic differences through the content, instructional methods, and organizational structures adopted. The second has more subtle roots and, as of this writing, has not been fully recognized.

In many ways the backroom talk of teachers and school administrators resembles the creative efforts of playwrights, actors, and others in the fine arts. On the basis of a few experiences with an ethnic group, gathered without the benefit of carefully developed methods of observation and filtered through one's own subjective way of looking at behavior, school personnel make stereotypic generalizations, which they pass on to their colleagues. In the fine arts, such generalizations may be more sensitive and more reflective of ethnic truths. In either case, the stereotypes generated remain undocumented by rational or scientific exploration. What a handful of college students and I proposed was to develop objective ways of doing what the fine arts and school teachers had done subjectively for so long.

The heart of an ethnic study is the stereotype. If a stereotype is based on overgeneralizations developed haphazardly and with scarce empirical data, it is obviously offensive to the ethnic group it describes. Even if a stereotype is developed with scholarly care, but remains unrevised for several years, it becomes an inaccurate representation of a group's ethnicity and, thus, offensive to the group it purports to describe. My initial goal was to achieve objective, empirically based, continually revised stereotypes, or, as I later called them, "ethnic profiles."

In undertaking the development of ethnic profiles, I tried to come to terms with all the many doubts I had about being able to achieve a valid description of a group's ethnicity by incorporating into the format of my study a mode of "ongoing tentativeness." The generalizations derived from the data collected were *never* to be considered more than hypotheses that could be tested and retested by applying them in lesson plans or classroom management. Furthermore, the study of any ethnic group would be continuous in nature, that is, perpetually seeking new data so that a dynamic revision of generalizations would occur as part of the descriptive phase as well as during periods of in-class application.

While I resigned myself to not being a scientific researcher and hoping, at best, for rational objectivity, I did not give up thoughts of being able to use my tentative generalizations to improve my teaching capabilities in multi-ethnic public school situations. I knew I needed the help of colleagues and that we would have to do a lot of comparing of our observations. I chose to call this "action research" and, with my doctorate in hand, I led a number of pre-service student teachers through my first faltering efforts at developing an ethnic profile of a minority group.

FOOTNOTES

[1]Celia S. Heller, *Mexican American Youth: Forgotten Youth at the Crossroads* (New York: Random House, 1966).

[2]Daryl J. Bem, *Beliefs, Attitudes, and Human Affairs* (Belmont, Calif.: Brooks/Cole Publishing Company, 1970) p. 8.

CHAPTER II

Ethnicity: What Have We Stumbled Into?

Whenever ethnic differences are discussed today, one of two images usually comes to mind. The pleasanter involves a multicultural festival of some kind in which the quaint foods or dress or whatever of several "exotic" groups are presented in some pleasing fashion for public display. The other less agreeable image is that of poverty-stricken minorities trapped in the ghettoes of America's cities. In both instances, it is almost as if ethnicity were assumed to be a phenomenon that applies *only* to Puerto Ricans or blacks or Appalachians.

Indeed, while talking to a young Chicano woman about my own ethnicity, I felt sincerely offended at the surprise she expressed that I, too, might be an ethnic. It was as though a part of my humanness had been ignored because I was not a member of a politically obvious minority group and thus could be relegated to the "Anglos" regardless of my actual ethnic history. In a sense, it was the melting pot syndrome in reverse. Large minority groups struggling out of very real socioeconomic difficulties today have impressed their sense of cultural uniqueness on the rest of us, and the "rest of us" seem to have become amorphously melted together into one thick soup.

While my reaction to this amorphous state was personal as well as emotional ("Hey, stop the world, I want my heritage back!"), it held significance for me as an educator. A few well-funded research projects have been making highly publicized

efforts to describe, say, Chicano ethnic traits, while ignoring the
ethnic traits of, for instance, middle-class Jewish or Anglo-Sax-
on teachers who often comprise large segments of a school
district's tenured teaching force. We have done almost nothing
about helping teachers to explore their own ethnicities and to
develop the self-awareness necessary if comparing ethnic traits
is to go beyond "quaintness" to usefulness in the classroom.

With all the talk about ethnicity, multi-cultural diversity, national differences, and the like, it would seem reasonable to expect to find some clear-cut definitions of the terms. What I
found was not very different from the usage of the terms I have
employed in the first few pages of this volume—"ethnicity" is
often loosely interchanged with "culture" and "nationality,"
while the term "race" is less in favor but sometimes included (to
add to the confusion). As a one-time journalist, I suspect much
of the looseness in terminology is a writer's effort to avoid repe-
titious usage of the same words. To a journalist producing an
interesting article for fleeting perusal in a daily paper, the in-
terchange of terminology presents no real difficulties. For me,
struggling to understand the ethnic traits of different groups
present in the public schools, including those of teachers, and
hoping to use my data in practical ways, the limits or parame-
ters of what I was going to study had to be reasonably clear. If
a systematic study of ethnic behaviors is to be undertaken, the
kind of data to be included and the kind to be excluded need to
be specified beforehand. Otherwise, the subjective interests of
the researchers—the behaviors that catch their fancy—will arbi-
trarily dominate the study.

DEFINING ETHNICITY

In our initial efforts at Indiana University, 1969-70, and the
University of Illinois, 1970-72, my students and I reviewed the
descriptions of America's largest minority groups as presented
in magazines, newspapers, encyclopedias, edited collections,
and other publications. We concentrated on shorter pieces be-

cause we thought a more complete cross section of how groups were described could be obtained and managed within the confines of a normal semester. We were struck by the similarity of a number of the characteristics attributed to quite different ethnic groups. For instance, we found that the extended family, i.e., a large number of individuals living together who are related to each other in various ways, was a descriptive term used for Appalachian, Chicano, black, and Puerto Rican Americans. These same groups were also described as being "outdoor-oriented," i.e., spending a large portion of their social lives outside of their homes in the outdoors or on the city streets. While I could not help but feel that knowledge of these traits was important to understanding how people behave, I reacted much as I did to Celia Heller's book on Mexican American youth. The fact that a group of people are outdoor-oriented tells me little about the specific ways they interact with each other while outside or about their attitudes toward meeting friends on the street as compared to their attitudes toward meeting friends in someone's home.

Traits such as extended family and outdoor orientation can serve to organize observations of the ways in which groups act under certain sets of conditions, but, taken alone, they are at a level of generalization that glosses over the actual kinds of behavior people engage in while they are outside or while they are sharing a household with numerous relatives. How does an Appalachian feel about her or his extended family? How does she or he behave toward aunts and cousins? Is it the same way a Neopolitan Italian feels or acts while living in her or his extended family?

Questions such as these helped me to formulate a distinction between culture and ethnicity[1] that was to prove not only reasonably helpful in our efforts to study specific ethnic groups but powerful in offering a new perspective on human behavior.

To begin with, I hypothesized that the trait of an extended family, at least in the United States, could probably be traced back to poverty, to the financial inability to rent or build more than one house. Furthermore, orientation toward the outdoors might also be attributed to the lack of space often prevalent in very poor homes. If ten people are living in a four-room apartment, it is more than likely that friends have to meet outside. This tells very little about the feelings, attitudes, and interpersonal activities typifying friendship.

It occurred to me that one could speak of the culture of poverty (as, indeed, has been done frequently) as a general, even an international, phenomenon. People follow similar patterns because they do not have the means to do otherwise. People are universally capable of culture, and what they do culturally may be limited by circumstances that are very general in scope. It is entirely possible that an automobile worker in Detroit will follow the exact procedures as one in San Francisco or Tokyo. Industrialization carries with it many similar, highly influential circumstances that lead people to act in ways that are generally similar without necessarily changing their more intimate ways of behaving. Are Japanese workers proud of what they are doing? How do Detroit workers feel about what they are doing? What are the cues that tell workers they are doing a good job? How do workers relate to each other successfully? The way things are done, the goals that become attached to them, and the manner in which they are accepted and related to other portions of our lives tend to be individually developed phenomena largely influenced by our relationships with the people around us and our need for social reinforcement.

Thus, I found myself making a distinction between the general circumstances of a group that contribute, in broad and imprecise brush strokes, to the major patterns of activities followed by that group and the more intimate ways of behaving that arise within a group as a result of family-neighborhood-peer interaction. It is, however, important to recognize that the more general and the more intimate ways of behaving are all part of culture. Culture is whatever people do to nature; what is not "natural" is "cultural."[2] All human beings have within them a cultural capacity; they are capable of creating what is not present in nature, they can imitate their peers, and they can adapt to or manipulate the circumstances of their environment.

My students and I obviously could not study all culture. What was important to me, an educator, seemed to be related primarily to the more intimate aspects of cultural development. How do youngsters feel about learning? Are their learning styles uniquely personal phenomena or do they contain traits emanating from membership in a particular group? Are my efforts at communicating with them really understood? Are my expectations for their behavior in my classroom consistent with the expectations they have encountered at home or among close friends? In other words, my major concerns were with that part of the cultural phenomenon arising from the interaction of each individual's cultural capacity with the traits of the members of his or her immediate circle, family first, then neighbors and peers.

I was really dealing with the earliest stages of cultural development that children go through. Children are not in full command of their intellectual powers when they are acquiring early cultural traits. It must be kept in mind that the onset of the human being's abstract thinking powers occurs somewhere between the ages of ten and twelve. Prior to this stage, children have only a limited capacity to judge the ways of behaving that they are absorbing. The way they address an adult, how they say their sentences, even when they smile are shaped "at gut level" long before they know what they are doing.

As my students and I mulled through these various ideas, we came to realize that we had stumbled upon a definition of ethnicity that held important implications for studies of human behavior far beyond our own limited efforts. *Ethnicity is that portion of cultural development that occurs before the individual is in complete command of his or her abstract intellectual powers and that is formed primarily through the individual's early contacts with family, neighbors, friends, teachers, and others, as well as with his or her immediate environment of the home and neighborhood.* Individuals will eventually attain some intellectual control over their ethnically learned behaviors, but that control is likely to remain incomplete. Much of what is learned ethnically is done at a very low level of awareness and in a way that seems to sidestep rationality.

All of us in our adult lives continue to do things for which we have no rational basis but for which we have a gut level need to continue doing. Let me give a somewhat exaggerated example to make my point. I see no real reason for wearing clothes in 90 degree weather. Given our present movie, stage, and magazine standards, I do not even believe that present sex mores logically support the continued wearing of clothing under very warm conditions. However, I would not and I could not walk around in public stark naked. To do so, would involve so much of my emotional energy that I would be unable to deal rationally with other ethnically absorbed traits that more urgently need my rational scrutiny. There is a limited capability within each of us to modify the ethnic traits we absorbed as children. We may change our accent or the way we smile but we cannot, intellectually or emotionally, change the multitude of traits that would have to be altered to change our basic ethnicity.

The perception of ethnicity as that part of cultural development occurring prior to the onset of one's abstract intellectual powers and as a result of one's direct contacts with people and the immediate environment led me to a number of other, admittedly speculative, considerations. Sociologists have long used the concept of "role" to distinguish the various sets of activities and responsibilities assumed by individuals throughout their lives. A politician may assume the roles of father, son, voter, consumer, or investor, depending on the circumstances; a G.M. worker may take on the roles of union organizer, mother, daughter, and so on. We all participate in numerous roles. Though I lack the means to verify the importance, it seems to me that the period of life during which a role is assumed is of immense importance and has been glossed over sociologically for too long. There are roles that are ethnically learned, i.e., absorbed prior to the period between the ages of ten and twelve, such as those between daughter and father, and there are roles rationally and consciously assumed in one's adulthood such as those of a G.M. worker and a union organizer. The control we have over our actions in these diverse roles may depend, to a considerable extent, on when in our cultural development these roles were assumed. Most of us do things in our roles as sons and daughters that we feel are useless or even silly, but we feel better, more content when we have done them. In our roles as workers, we may do things we cannot support rationally, for instance, we may rationally blame our need for a pay check for engaging in activities we believe are senseless. However, we will not feel better for having done them—relieved perhaps, but not better!

SCHOLASTIC ETHNICITY

This distinction of when roles are assumed naturally in a person's life led to an examination of the role of the student. Our children enter school by the age of five or six (many even earlier), and they spend a significant portion of the next twelve years in them not merely "book learning," but playing, eating, fighting, hurting, striving, hoping, and so on. The public school bureaucracy and its traditions are encountered by students before they are able to judge their quality. Modes of communication, of acceptable relationships between students, teachers, and administrators, of praiseworthy attitudes, and of reward and punishment are presented to children before they have the intellectual power or the sociological perspective to reject them.

The role of student is fundamentally different from many other roles assumed in life. It is absorbed at such an early date in individuals' formations and permeates so much of their early existence that logic cannot overcome the patterns of behavior thus intimately assimilated. The roles of automobile worker, consumer, or executive, are assimilated quite differently, for while they are being assumed, adults have command of their abstract, logical reasoning abilities as well as some command of available choices.

Learning to be a student has many of the characteristics of learning to be a member of an ethnic group. A whole way of living is assimilated both from one's family life and from one's school life. The family way may not be at all like the scholastic way—or there may be many points of similarity and compatibility. In any case, youngsters are unaware of what is happening to them. By the age of ten or eleven American students have at least two ethnicities: that of their heritage and that of their school.

Furthermore, scholastic ethnicity is likely to be a national phenomenon because the bureaucracy and the traditions of the public schools, local control notwithstanding, are very similar throughout the nation *as well as across several generations.* The form and uses of grading, despite long arguments to the contrary, have remained essentially unchanged for generations from one end of the nation to the other. The content of study has changed only minimally, and when it has changed, it has been primarily in recognition that new knowledge has been acquired. It is the rare high school graduate who has not studied the amoeba or had a survey course in English literature, unless a nonacademic program is followed in which other such predictable subjects as "shop" are studied. A uniform number of periods per day, bells, hall monitors, and even required notes for absences still predominate. Bureaucracies are not likely to change in significant ways, and the school bureaucracy is not an exception.

Scholastic ethnicity, which in many ways is modeled by this bureaucracy, has shown remarkable stability. Indeed, while it has not essentially changed for generations, the ethnicities of different cultural groups have been significantly influenced by new, quite general circumstances such as enormously increased mobility, readily available mastermind computers, fear of worldwide pollution, and other factors. It may well be, given the greater stability of scholastic ethnicity, that there is no American ethnic group whose traits significantly resemble those assimilated during the public school experience. The alienation so many American students have felt in the public school may be caused by the increasing distance between the ethnicity of their heritage and the scholastic ethnicity that they begin to acquire around the age of five. In other words, the problems of incompatability between scholastic ethnicity and the ethnicity of one's heritage may extend far beyond a few minority groups into the heart of America's majorities.

If significant changes have not happened in the public schools, it certainly has not been for lack of effort. Most of the efforts, however, have not taken into account the emotional, "gut-level" power of scholastic ethnicity. A class of students, regardless of their age level, who have assimilated their roles well at the pre-abstract stages of intellectual development are really not able to modify their ways of acting simply because a sincere, idealistic young teacher stands before them more or less saying, "Let's act differently"—even if students think the young teacher is right! Students feel an almost insurmountable need to know exactly what is expected of them—How many pages should they read? How long should the report be? If they are told to choose their own topic for study and to decide for themselves on the kinds of activities to be undertaken, the sense of disorientation, especially among college-oriented high school students, often leads to the brink of classroom rebellion. If the threat of grades is removed, the likelihood of overt rebellion lessens, but most students tend to over relax and perform at levels significantly below their capacities. Indeed, "good students" probably make their greatest efforts in courses where they risk a low grade. It is usually not long before the idealistic young teacher reverts to the expected patterns of behavior traditionally followed in the public schools because that is the most productive route for students in terms of tangible achievements.

If change is to occur in the public schools, the nature of scholastic ethnicity must be dealt with as it develops during the pre-abstract, intellectual stages of childhood. Teachers (and, yes, public school administrators!) need to understand not only the behaviors of their own and their students' ethnic heritages, but behaviors reflecting scholastic ethnicity. Rational control of grading, attendance requirements, standardized testing, and the like presently escape us because not only do students and school personnel actively possess scholastic ethnicity, but so, too, do the parents of students and the public at large.

AN AMERICAN ETHNICITY

The definition of ethnicity that my students and I adopted for our studies led us to ask whether there was anything like a general American ethnicity, that is, a set of ethnically learned behaviors that are shared by most Americans regardless of their individual heritages. The traits of scholastic ethnicity do have a national sphere of influence and could be a part of a general American ethnicity (if it exists at all), despite the schools' bureaucratic system, whose scholastic traditions have been modified very little since the 1930s while America's traditions have changed significantly.

We had little doubt that there was an American cultural experience. The innumerable hamburger stands, thousands of miles of highway, millions of cars, appliances, and other types of mass-produced machinery create broadly shared experiences that lead to an American culture easily distinguished from that of Mexico or many European countries (although, in the latter instance, the increasing similarity of mass production is tending to produce a broader, international rubric—the industrial-technological culture). These nationally experienced phenomena usually filter through to young children via the adults with whom they are in direct contact, normally members of their family. Different ethnic groups share in an American culture insofar as they must react to similar phenomena. Young children know and learn these reactions long before they have any grasp of their broader implications. Thus, it is possible to say that while there are significant ethnic differences among American blacks and other American ethnic groups, American blacks are culturally closer to these groups than to the blacks of Ethiopia or Nigeria.

What brought us to the consideration of an American ethnicity was the expanding phenomenon of mass communication. Television, in particular, became the object of our discussions. Clearly, television is a nationally shared, cultural circumstance of American life. By its very nature, however, it also has a significant place in the ethnic environment of a young child's home. It has been estimated that the average pre-schooler watches television somewhere between five and eight hours per day. This means that children are involved with and listening to a great number of people, who often are not of their own ethnic group, for a considerable portion of their waking hours and while they are still in the pre-abstract stages of intellectual development. Furthermore, although some adult filtering may occur, the experience of television is primarily a direct one, with children reacting to the content of television programs much as they might to their own firsthand experiences. The kinds of learning in which children engage while watching television, given the definition we had accepted, seem to have the characteristics of ethnic assimilation.

Before the advent of public television, while radio and other forms of mass communication such as the cinema were well established, the black sociologist W. E. B. Dubois was keenly aware of a sense of duality that plagued the black world: "One ever feels his twoness—an American, a Negro, two souls, two thoughts, two unreconciled strivings . . . ."[3] The duality referred to by Dubois could be the development of dual ethnic heritages, both contained within the general experiences of the American-cultural scene but one a direct derivative of personal interactions and the other a result of impersonal contacts by mass communication entering the world of children during the ethnic stages of their development. Because children's immediate families or friends do not act as intermediaries filtering the input of television before it reaches them, we did not feel it or other mass media could be assigned to the general American cultural experience. Ethnic groups do make adaptations to their cultural circumstances that eventually do filter through to children. However, the message and the effect of television is direct, immediate, and of a dramatic power certainly comparable to children's firsthand experiences.

The ethnic map that was beginning to form as we explored possible outcomes of our definition was complex far beyond expectation. As we saw it, there was the possibility that children of ten could be the bearers, simultaneously, of their familys' ethnic heritage, an American ethnic heritage, and a national, scholastic ethnicity.

UTILIZING THE DEFINITION

Although it was obviously beyond our capacity to verify empirically our hypotheses regarding the several distinct ethnicities borne by the average American, the definition did help us to determine the kinds of data that we would consider "ethnic data." Statements such as, "The first relatively large black migration into Michigan began about 1840"[4] and "One of the striking features of the Mexican American group is that its population is young. Its median age is close to 20, as compared with about 30 years for the total U.S. white population,"[5] were not considered ethnic data, even though they were of cultural significance.

The questions we asked about such statements were based on our definition of ethnicity: Would young children be directly influenced by this data? Would they actually observe it, react, or see reactions to it? Would they be likely to have any identifiable experiences prior to the onset of their abstract thinking powers resulting directly from the data presented? Quite possibly, the higher number of youths present in a child's environment might be an influential ethnic factor. However, we felt that this possible influence had to be surmised while too many related variables were unknown. For instance, were teenage siblings encouraged to be with younger children or were they cut off from other children after the onset of puberty? In sum, we felt that the statements noted above gave neither directly pertinent information about the kinds of behaviors youngsters would be expected to engage in or would be likely to encounter from their family and peers, nor expanded on the nature of their environment in a way that would add to an ethnic study as opposed to a study dealing with general cultural circumstances shared by many ethnic groups.

On the other hand, the following statement discussing the symbolic importance of dress in an Amish community was considered to contain ethnic data according to our definition of ethnicity:

> The hat, for example, distinguishes the Amish man from the outsider and also symbolizes his role within his social structure. When the two-year-old boy discards a dress and begins wearing trousers for the first time, he also receives a stiff jet-black hat with three or more inches of brim.[6]

A two-year-old boy must surely be deeply impressed by being given a hat and pants similar to those of his father, which are not given to his sister who still wears a dress. What might it mean to a six-or seven-year-old Amish student if his teacher asked him *not* to wear his hat in the school building? Perhaps nothing because in his ethnic group it may be usual for males to remove their hats whenever they are in a building. On the other hand, that may not be the case, and a teacher's apparently simple request could undermine the boy's image of his own social acceptability. In the case of the Amish, whose refusal to accept modern conveniences as well as their "quaint" dress have long emphasized their religious diversity, the teacher is likely to ask about the significance attached to black hats before forbidding a boy to wear his hat to class. That very same teacher might not hesitate an instant to order a black American to remove a hat he had worn to class. There is all too frequently an assumption that wearing a hat to class means the same to the student as it does to the teacher.

Another example of ethnic data is the following statement concerning the way Southwestern American Indian children learn from adults:

> A reluctance to try too soon and the accompanying fear of being "shamed" if one does not succeed may account for the seemingly passive, uninterested, and unresponsive attitude of Indian students . . . A Navajo girl, for instance, is said to watch her mother weaving rugs for a very long time before she asks for a loom. She then produces a small rug of marketable quality at the local trading post.[7]

The author of this statement is not referring to one child's unique learning style; he is, rather, referring to a pattern of behavior observed among many Navajo children. Children do not try a number of times with an adult close by helping and correcting them. Instead, they observe an activity repeatedly, going over the performance in their heads, until they are certain that they will do the task well—at least before any kind of an audience—the very first time they undertake its performance. Compare this with the prevailing tendency of school teachers to help children by correcting them and encouraging them to try even if a few mistakes are made. There is obviously the possibility of considerable tension arising between Navajo children's ethnic heritage and scholastic ethnicity. The terrible shame and embarrassment Navajo children may have to cope with if they are forced to try publicly is not something they can control or even fully understand when, at the age of seven or eight, their teacher insists that they at least show a willingness to learn.

The data we decided to classify as ethnic generally reflected types of behaviors that could be observed either happening to or being performed by young children mostly during their contacts with family, friends, and teachers. Even descriptions of feelings and beliefs were to be directly related to specific activities, i.e., wearing a hat, learning a task, or kneeling in church. It was not ethnic data to say that children are respectful toward adults. Some specific description of a behavior repeated by many youngsters of a group would have to be linked to the idea of respect to have ethnic rather than broadly cultural data. We persistently asked of the data we found, "How would this influence the behavior of children prior to the onset of their abstract, intellectual powers?"

FOOTNOTES

[1]Anthropologists and sociologists have long struggled with the nature of ethnicity without, however, coming to any real consensus. In my article, "Learning Style: the Ethnic Factor," *Education Research Quarterly,* Winter 1978, I review some of these definitions and indicate where the definition I finally used differs from all those I have encountered.

[2]The anthropologist David Bidney, prior to his retirement, offered this proposition to his classes at Indiana University.

[3]W. E. B. Dubois, *The Souls of Black Folk,* (New York: Fawcett Publications, (paperback, 1961,) p. 17.

[4]*Detroit Free Press,* December 8, 1973, p. 1B.

[5]Celia S. Heller, *Mexican American Youth: Forgotten Youth at the Crossroads* (New York: Random House, 1966) p. 27

[6]John A. Hostetler, *Amish Society,* rev. ed. Baltimore: Johns Hopkins University Press, 1968, paperback 1970, p. 135.

[7]Sirarpi Ohannessian, *The Study of the Problems of Teaching English to American Indians,* (Washington, D. C.: Center for Applied Linguistics, July 1967) p. 13.

CHAPTER III

Aspects of Ethnicity

Establishing a definition of ethnicity helped us to think through what we were about and where we might be going, but it was not enough. If constructs for the objective study of ethnicity were to be devised, more than definitions were needed. The amount of ethnic data that could be collected about any one group was mind-boggling. How would we collect this data so that we could also retrieve it with some efficiency when it was needed? How, too, could our observations be collected so that they might be compared and contrasted with the data collected by other observers? This was particularly important since we hoped to achieve ethnic profiles that were composites of observations made by different individuals and derived from diverse sources.

We were also concerned with gathering a complete gamut of ethnic information for our profiles. We did not want our subjective interests to determine the kinds of ethnic data we would observe for we felt it important to the validity of our profiles to include observations of all the major kinds of ethnic behaviors that we could conceive. This meant that we had to make a plan of what we were going to look for and how we were going to store and retrieve what we found. In the words of the social scientist Abraham Kaplan: "There are always many ways of mapping behavior into data. . . . But without some mapping or other, the process of observation is of no scientific significance."[1]

Furthermore, whatever plan we adopted, it would eventually need to take into account the uses that were to be made of the data. Our goal was to assist teachers of multi-ethnic classrooms in improving their instructional methodology and interpersonal relations with students. In such a context, it would make little sense to organize, say, data regarding values according to the type of political institution within which the observations were made, although such an approach might be very productive if the goal were to gain greater insight into the compatability of institutional arrangements with the values held by the people served. The plan for our data would have to reflect present public school-classroom circumstances.

To achieve valid and objectively defensible profiles, we undertook an analysis of the various aspects of ethnicity implicit in our definition. What were the major kinds of behavior children might acquire as a result of their contacts with their immediate environment, including, of course, the people upon whom they depended for their biological survival and/or emotional well-being? This question helped us eliminate such phenomena as physical growth, for although environment does influence children's growth, it is not an acquired behavior. Rubrics such as transportation did not fit as well into the acquired behaviors of childhood as they did into general cultural experiences normally filtered through adults before they influence children's behavior. We also considered such categories as eating habits, which we all agreed would include many ethnically-acquired behaviors, but we decided that it was, in scope, too narrow a category. It might, subsequently, become a useful subcategory, but its adoption as a major aspect of ethnic behavior would only clutter our profile.

If a geographic map of a state were to list in bold type every town having a population of 5,000 or more, the map would become far less useful for most people. Likewise, if there were many categories for ethnic behavior with almost no differentiation for scope and importance, the very number of categories requiring equal attention would interfere with a teacher's ability to use the data collected. There would just be too many similar labels for the human mind to cope with efficiently. Furthermore, since we were trying to develop categories embracing all the major kinds of behaviors acquired during childhood, it was our belief that most narrow rubrics would be subsumed under such major categories, if these succeeded in covering the complete range of ethnicity.

In the end, we came up, hesitantly, with five categories that we believe are five major aspects of ethnicity. While we tried to include all possible ethnic behaviors, the effort was a heuristic one, and we cannot be sure that it is fully successful. We also attempted to achieve aspects that are reasonably distinct from each other. We, of course, realized that people engage in a whole gamut of behaviors simultaneously and that one observation might be classified under several categories. Our goal was to achieve categories so clearly distinct from each other that they could be useful in analyzing a simultaneously enacted set of ethnic behaviors. Again, we cannot be sure that we have fully succeeded.

AN OVERVIEW OF THE FIVE ASPECTS OF ETHNICITY

Following are the aspects of ethnicity that eventually were adopted as the bases for our ethnic profiles:

> Verbal Communication
> Nonverbal Communication
> Orientation Modes
> Social Value Patterns
> Intellectual Modes

Each of the aspects was investigated further. We tried to find out what kinds of studies had already been done in these areas and, then, how we could make direct observations of our own. We developed for each aspect a set of subcategories to serve as a guide or specialized map for our own studies of that aspect.

A brief explanation of the kinds of behavior covered by each aspect might be useful at this point. We divided the phenomena of communication into two aspects—verbal and nonverbal. All behaviors acquired during early childhood that involve the human voice* in group-oriented forms of communication were classified as verbal. Behaviors that are not vocal but involve movements of the human body or other kinds of physical arrangements to communicate and that are learned in the pre-abstract stages of intellectual development were classified as nonverbal.

The intent to communicate may not be fully conscious on the parts of either the transmittor or the receiver of the message. Generally there seems to be more awareness of the intent to communicate when behaviors are vocalized and less awareness when body movements are involved. We noted, with some surprise, that we were continually moving our hands while we were speaking *without realizing it* and that we actually felt the need to move our hands at certain points of our discussion. When we tried to keep our hands still, it was as though some significant meaning had been excluded from what we were saying. We also came to realize that we did many things with our voices while speaking that were quite unconscious but that did carry intentional meaning. We talked more quickly or more slowly or with longer pauses according to the impressions we were trying to communicate. Awareness of the intent to communicate, however, is not a necessary characteristic for these two categories. What is necessary is an identifiable, repeated behavior having a reasonably similar meaning for all the members of an ethnic group and used for purposes of communicating with others.

The third category, orientation modes, was developed after we had used the nonverbal communication category for a while. We came to realize that people frequently engage in acquired, nonverbal behaviors, including certain patterns of body movements, *without any intention of communicating.* As individuals, independently of any direct contact with others, we go on relat-

*Note: Written language, which is directly based on oral language, is classified as verbal communication.

ing to our environment in ways that are ethnically learned. At first, we engage in these nonverbal ways of dealing with the environment by imitating the ways others act under similar circumstances. As time goes on, these ways become intimately part of us and are no longer dependent on the presence of other people. They are our ways of dealing with or orienting ourselves to our surroundings. For instance, we may be watching television without anyone else around and we will still sit in certain predictable positions that are more comfortable to us than other positions typically found in the relaxation behaviors of other ethnic groups. We expect and want our bed linens to be bright (if not white) and such rational considerations as cleanliness are not really part of this expectation; we simply do not feel comfortable at the thought of sleeping on black linen. Even the eating habits we acquire, which are sometimes used as expressions of socioeconomic class, often fall under the ethnic aspect of orientation modes. For example, in a situation devoid of social interaction—no one else is present—one is likely to set the table as usual or cut meat in the American style, which involves resting the knife on the plate after the meat has been cut and transferring the fork to the right hand before finally eating the morsel of meat. It would be more efficient to simply cut up all the meat at once and then eat it, but how many of us do that even when we are alone?

The primary characteristic of orientation modes is the lack of intended interaction with others either by communication or by following accepted social patterns reflecting the group's values. Because interaction wih others is excluded, most of the behaviors under this category are nonverbal. The question we asked in looking for orientation modes was how do individuals behave in their environment when it is devoid of or somehow ignores other people? This means that many behaviors, which are social in origin but eventually become so intimate a part of an individual's way of dealing with her or his world that she or he persists in using them in nonsocial situations, would be classified as orientation modes.

The aspect of social value patterns refers to the behavioral patterns of people as members of their ethnic group. These are behaviors that reflect the values of the group as a whole. Marriage and divorce and the ways these are allowed to happen are examples. Involvement in ceremonies of various kinds, from attending a funeral to saluting a flag, may take on special meanings personally, but they remain primarily public functions and reflect the efforts of individual ethnic members to meet the expectations of their group. Such expectations may also include being a good father or a good son as well as being a good worker.

Patterns of social behavior may be valued in different degrees and ways by the group ranging from desirable-acceptable to undesirable-unacceptable, from important to unimportant, and from possible to impossible. Values are often not expressed openly and, indeed, often exist in contradiction with each other as well as at different levels of awareness. What is prized may not be consistent with what is considered morally ideal. For example, an ethnic group may overtly praise marital fidelity as a moral ideal while covertly encouraging men to prize "manliness" as demonstrated by the many women they have known intimately. What is more, a man may not have anything like the sexual drive he believes is socially prized and therefore desirable, and may even lie to build an image that is not at all consistent with the morally ideal image of a faithful husband. Both moral ideals and prizings operate in social value patterns.

The relationship of the values of the group developed in the individual with the values of the group sustained publicly for all members of the group both intrigued and overwhelmed us. How do individually held values of a group member relate to group-held values? It was clear that whatever descriptions we would achieve in this area would be insufficient and that great precautions had to be taken to avoid gross overgeneralizations. As with the other aspects, our position was that the effort to make objective, organized observations was better than haphazard, impressionistic observations that now dominate the ethnic data used by teachers. We hoped that the development of a series of subcategories, which would make the nature of what we were looking for more precise, would help us over some of the pitfalls.

The aspect of intellectual modes deals primarily with how people have learned to learn, i.e., their learning styles, as well as their attitudes toward learning and toward what is learned. It is important to emphasize that intellectual traits of an innate, biological nature (if such exist) are intentionally not included in this category, although, admittedly, innate intellectual capacities have not yet been successfully separated from the influences that ethnicity has on intellectual development. In other words, whenever a standardized I.Q. test is administered to youngsters it reflects, simultaneously, the intellectual potential with which the youngsters are born, the ethnic influences on their subsequent intellectual development, and, importantly, the cultural expectations for intellectual performance of whoever devised the test. Intellectual modes is concerned primarily with the ways in which childhood learnings are influenced by the ethnic environment. When children are learning, do adults tell them that they must deal with one problem at a time? Are they praised for knowing all the important dates of the Revolution or for being able to recite a poem? Is special stress given to their being successful in sports or playing a musical instrument? While some of the responses to questions such as these may reflect personality differences, a similarity of responses based on diverse individuals belonging to an ethnic group would suggest that the ethnic group had brought some influence to bear on the ways its young approach learning.

LIMITATIONS AND UNCERTAINTIES

At the risk of being tedious, I feel the limitations of using these five aspects of ethnicity to achieve valid and objectively defensible ethnic profiles must be reiterated. Because ethnic development is a part of cultural development, there is often considerable vagueness in the boundaries between broadly cultural phenomena and ethnic characteristics. Our hypothesis that there is an American ethnicity as well as ethnicities of individual heritage that exist within a general environment of American culture seems to make the boundaries even fuzzier. The development of five categories of ethnic behaviors does not diminish these grey areas of uncertainty.

For the most part, our profiles depend on data obtained from diverse kinds of observations of numerous subjects by observers of various backgrounds. Eliminating some observations as being of a personal rather than ethnic quality is an important factor, which is only possible as the frequency of observations of a given ethnic group increases and the incidences of specific kinds of occurrences are found to be low and sporadic. There is, however, an inherent weakness, which must be noted, in this technique of surveying-comparing diverse observations. Much of what is observed in human activity may be repeated only rarely, or, for that matter, never again. Circumstances combine uniquely to produce unrepeatable situations. As Kaplan so aptly emphasized: "Many important scientific observations take place on special occasions whose recurrence is incidental to their scientific significance. Of particular importance to behavioral science are special events like clinical outbursts, disasters, and war crises, as well as regularly recurrent ones like elections or rain dances . . ."[2] What this means for our study is that certain ethnic traits, because of their infrequency of occurrence, may be mistakenly thought of as personality traits or may be missed altogether even though they are significant for the ethnic group being described. Giving birth is such an example.

Furthermore, while our goal was to achieve categories of ethnic behavior that were distinct from each other, that very goal poses a problem for the validity of our studies. Human development is based on sets of integrated phenomena that cannot be separated from each other. We, on the other hand, have tried to take an important part of human development— ethnicity—and analyze it into separate parts, the five aspects. Of

course, the separation is useful as an objective guide for observations and data collection. However, to obtain that usefulness, we give up a certain validity in the representation of
human development for the separateness of the categories mis-
represents the integratedness of the phenomena under study. It
also means that the very same data will sometimes have to be
classified under more than one category. For instance, in one
observation it was noted that a boy asked many questions about
what he was learning even during the initial approach to that
learning when the teacher was introducing the basic ideas. Asking many questions during the initial learning period is both a
form of verbal communication and a characteristic of learning
style. There may even be a special social context that makes
questioning behaviors desirable. The very same observation
might have to be noted for each of three aspects with the only
modification being one of emphasis, possibly as in the
following:

Verbal communication - A young student engages in asking many questions of his teach-
er during an introductory lesson.

Social value pattern - It is considered socially desirable for the young student to
ask many questions of his
teacher during an introductory
lesson.

Intellectual modes - The young student asks many
questions while at the initial
stages of learning a new unit.

Of course with such a simple example, it would seem that making three separate inputs from a single instance is multiplying
complexity rather than achieving simplicity. What must be remembered is that there will be many such extracted inputs under each category coming from a variety of sources. Thus, while

questioning as part of a learning style might be subsequently confirmed, the social desirability of such questioning might not —indeed, it might be very undesirable.

Generally the five aspects of ethnicity are five views or perspectives of human behavior indicative of one or another emphasis that a behavior carries. Any intent to communicate will tend to reflect a social value pattern. However, *the aspect of verbal communication emphasizes how and what we communicate as opposed to the kinds of behaviors expected from us by our group and the values attributed to these behaviors by the group and by ourselves as members of the group.* Similarly, intellectual modes will frequently be found together with verbal communication; the emphasis there, however, is *on how and what we learn and not on how or what we say.* In a sense, the five aspects of ethnicity are ways of achieving specialized studies of ethnic behavior. They make it possible to focus on one type of behavior at a time to try to achieve generalizations about that behavior. The intent is to eventually bring these five categories together in some comparative or contrasting fashion. However, each category, taken alone, enables a researcher to limit the quantity and complexity of what is to be observed.

There are advantages and drawbacks in this kind of specialization. The study of grammar exemplifies how both the positive and the negative may be present; on the one hand, concentration on phenomena such as syntax, morphology, and phonology makes it possible to achieve models that can predict, with reasonable certainty, what sentences in a language will look or sound like; on the other hand, this very concentration leads us to believe that all verbal communication can be understood grammatically, or, at the very least, leads us to underestimate the significance of paralinguistic features such as stress and tempo. Indeed, there is a presently emerging field called the ethnography of speaking,[3] which is attempting to analyze all factors that contribute meaning to speech in a given setting. Socioeconomic class, age, sex, context, group rituals, and available repertoires of speaking behaviors are among the factors that would be considered in the analysis of a single act such as a greeting or engaging in conversation. In essence, the specialization has shifted to the act, the description of which tends to become complete though quite complex.

Because I am so intensely aware of the limitations inherent in the development of five aspects of ethnicity, I have had to face the question of whether what is gained is worth the drawbacks. Emphasizing major activities such as getting married, entering school, and the like was certainly a possible way of organizing our study. Emphasizing activities, however, tended to bring ethnic and generally cultural behaviors together, which, while reflecting reality, does little to help us understand the different ways we think and behave because we grew up with one ethnic group instead of another. This is especially true when we, as a pluralistic society, participate in some generally shared activity such as banking or schooling. Why do adult students continue to interrupt during a learning situation even though it offends a majority of the other students? Perhaps they simply have an offensive or deviant personality. On the other hand, it may well be a behavior they acquired ethnically and is now an intimate part of the way they learn. Even if told of the behavior, they may not be able to control their actions. They are, after all, still reinforced in the behavior by their ethnic group. To study the influence of ethnicity, it seemed important to achieve some generalized descriptions about behaviors acquired during childhood rather than a picture of all the different phenomena that could influence the meaning of a specific (though representative) act such as a greeting.

Observations oriented toward types of ethnic behaviors were useful to me as a teacher in my Gary, Indiana, classroom. If I found myself reacting negatively or ineffectively to several members of an ethnic group, I would look for the behaviors that seemed to make me most uncomfortable. Were there miscues in our communication system or points of significant diversity in our social value patterns? What was I not understanding? Once I had zeroed in on a behavioral area, I tried to develop a description of my own ways of acting as well as to observe the students' ethnic group with this specific behavior in mind. Sometimes a solution meant lowering my voice or suppressing my own desire to push a youngster away who had come too close for *my* comfort but who was being no more than friendly. Sometimes it meant showing annoyance when I wasn't annoyed at all. This latter instance actually occurred when a black colleague pointed out to me that the black teenager who had rolled his eyes "a certain way" was really telling me to get off his back and stop bothering him. I had not noticed, but I did the next time it happened. When I told him not to roll his eyes at me, he was a little surprised and a little more willing to listen. But then, success in teaching is often made up of seemingly minor behavioral victories that add up to students being willing to learn.

FOOTNOTES

[1] Abraham Kaplan, *The Conduct of Inquiry: Methodology for Behavioral Science* (New York: Chandler Publishing Company, 1964) pp. 133-134.

[2] Ibid., p. 127.

[3] Linguists such as Dell Hymes, Allen Grimshaw, William Labov, J. J. Gumperz, and Susan Ervin-Tripp have been variously involved in trying to develop methods and organization in the "ethnography of speaking." For an in-depth presentation of the field see: *Explorations in the Ethnography of Speaking,* Richard Bauman and Joel Sherzer, ed. (New York: Cambridge University Press, 1974.)

CHAPTER IV

Verbal Communication

All languages have structure, and all people use structure when speaking. They may not be fully aware of how they organize their language—that is, what rules they follow—but they do follow rules with a high degree of accuracy. These rules are learned by children prior to the development of their abstract intellectual abilities as a result of their contacts with relatives, friends, and acquaintances. The capacity to learn oral language seems to be a universal capacity of mankind. Children normally manifest this universal capacity within the context of their environment, learning to speak while they are still unable to judge the various social qualities attached to what will become their native tongue.

By the age of five, most youngsters are reasonably competent in some form of oral speech. The language they have learned is suited for and adequate to their environment. No language can be superior or inferior but only different in the sense that it fits the needs of different groups. A child coming to school may speak a native tongue that is quite different from the standard English generally used in American schools. These differences may go well beyond simple dictionary definitions or diverse syntactical structures to the kinds of impressions youngsters give their teachers about their intellectual abilities, their attitudes, and even their social acceptability.

ETHNICITY IN BOTH LEARNING AND JUDGING SPEECH

I personally have not yet overcome the spontaneous reaction I seem to have to anyone who speaks English in ways still referred to as "incorrect." I have, moreover, become aware of certain differentiations that these gut reactions of mine seem to make unwittingly. A French person elongating the "i" sound in "this" (to "thhiiss") and using rather odd constructions such as, "Do you not think this is not so?" is rather pleasing to my ear, and I am usually disposed to listen more attentively and with a certain willingness to give weight to what he or she says. On the other hand, a Puerto Rican youngster who uses "dhe" for "the" and adds an extra negative such as, "I'm not doing nothing," tends to be downgraded in my mind. I understand what exaggerated assumptions I am making on the basis of insufficient verbal data, and I do try to disavow my impressions and to keep my mind open to all regardless of the language they speak. But it does bother me.

Why should I, supposedly an enlightened, sophisticated individual, react so simplistically? Obviously, it is not only children's language that is ethnic, but my reactions to their language. The fact that I can generalize about differences in my own reactions to the way people speak seems to indicate that I follow a set of rules, not merely about how to speak but about how to judge speech. Since, when I talk to friends about the impressions a youngster's speech gives me, they follow and often share my judgments, I am inclined to believe that there are shared sets of rules, learned ethnically, for judging speech as well as for speaking. If this is true, even to a limited extent, it means that I learned certain criteria for deciding about language before I was capable of evaluating the validity of the criteria. This might account for the struggle I normally engage in when my adult logic tells me that my reaction to someone's speech is unreasonable and that I need to keep an open mind (which sometimes results in my accepting the most patently foolish statements without a whimper).

Labov, in his investigation of New York speech and social status, isolated five phonological variables he found associated with diverse levels of social status. Sentences containing these phonological characteristics were recorded by different subjects, and listeners were asked to rate the subjects on an occupational scale. The occupational evaluation of the listeners correlated significantly with Labov's social status classification of the five variables.[1] In other words, the criteria for judging social status, which we all seem to have within us, is based in significant ways on how people sound to us as well as on how "correctly" they structure the spoken language.

As my students and I tried to examine further the bases upon which judgments about people's language are made, we came to recognize how deeply influenced we were by phonological variables not directly related to the pronounciation of words. The patterns of a speaker's pauses, the tempo of the speech, the stress given to certain parts of sentences, the pitch range of the sentences—all seem to influence judgment of a speaker without our really understanding how we use the criteria we are obviously following. Interestingly, very little attention is given to such considerations in the public school curriculum.

In part, this oversight may reflect how little we really understand about the way phonological patterns operate in the formation of listener impressions. Most of the time we are not even aware of the judgments we are making. For instance, how do the length of pauses and their position between as well as within sentences influence our reactions to a person socially? Would this differ in an intellectual context? What determines a "pleasant sounding" person? Are such reactions part of an American ethnicity or do they tend to reflect the diverse ethnicities of our pluralistic heritage? Most of all, given the action research approach proposed in this work, what are the most prominent phonological characteristics of the ethnic groups present in *my* classroom and what are *my* reactions, as teacher, to these characteristics? Once this latter question is dealt with honestly at the personal level, the ethnic aspect of language, i.e., its "gut-level-ness," can begin to be brought under some logical control and can become the object of some educational planning.

GRAMMATICAL STRUCTURE AND NONSTANDARD DIALECTS

My students and I rejected the theory that standard English (or standard any language) is superior to other dialects and therefore needs to be taught if a higher quality of schooling is to be achieved. We did, however, acknowledge that a public school needs to deal with the standard language and do some teaching of it. The question we faced was how to do that teaching while making cognitive use of the language models a child already knows and while expressing in our instructional activities the respect due all native tongues, whether they be standard or non-standard dialects.

Up until the mid-sixties, American educators acted upon the belief that standard English was a superior tongue, and studies have found that even teachers who were members of minority groups speaking nonstandard English dialects accepted this proposition.[2] A number of researchers supported the perception of standard English as superior, or, in the terminology of a period that labelled children of minority groups as *culturally deprived,* the theory of linguistic deficits giving rise to cognitive deficits. Bernstein, among the better known of these researchers, compared black English dialect with standard English and, because of short, less elaborate conversations in the former, labelled it "restricted" language.[3] The ethnocentric bias of this and similar generalizations has been repeatedly challenged. Linguist William Labov even took conversations similar to those analyzed by Bernstein and made the case that superior logical capacity was reflected by the black English dialect.[4]

The difference between viewing nonstandard dialects as inferior languages somehow representing cognitive deficits and viewing nonstandard dialects as reflecting differing communication needs is important for educators, especially for urban school teachers. From the former perspective, teachers have no need to understand the grammatical structure of a dialect since they will probably ignore the ethnically acquired oral communication system in favor of using and teaching standard English. From the latter perspective, dialects may be seen as cognitively adequate instruments of communication that can be used to increase the linguistic capacities of children. To use an ethnic dialect for increasing linguistic capacity would necessarily mean that teachers have to acquire some degree of competence in the grammatical structures of the dialect. Such competence could probably not be and need not be complete. Awareness of even a few structural features could be incorporated into a set of exercises that might help youngsters understand how, say, the future tense is systematically distinguished from the present.

In all frankness, most of the burden of achieving such dialectal competence falls almost completely on teachers. Dialects have been considered as inferior both socially and educationally for such an extended period that what little has been done has neither been directed toward increasing understanding of the nature of ethnic diversity nor toward possible educational benefits. The studies of Wolfram, Fasold, Stewart, Baratz, and others concerned with black English are of relatively recent vintage, dating to the mid- and late sixties for the most part. Enormous strides have been made in describing the structure of black English, and there is a growing effort to describe Appalachian English, especially under the auspices of Cratis D. Williams of Appalachian State University. However, the English dialects of America's large Spanish-speaking population have been dealt with only minimally. In this case, the expected brief existence of these dialects seems to be a deterrent to in-depth linguistic descriptions since assimilation of standard English is expected to occur within one or two generations. The "temporariness" of these dialects does not, however, render them any less ethnic in their influence nor any less important educationally.

A brief scenario of what happens to a recently "settled out" migrant Chicano's language might be helpful here in clarifying the importance of dialects educationally. Let's say that Carlo's family stopped following the crop harvests when he was four years old and settled down in an urban area populated by first- and second-generation Greek and Pakistanian Americans. His first native tongue is probably some variation of Spanish, quite different from the standard Spanish a teacher might have studied. With his family, he goes shopping and makes acquaintances in the neighborhood. The neighborhood is populated by three ethnic groups, who, though keeping to themselves, do increasingly interact with each other. An English dialect of sorts arises as the neighborhood language. It may disappear in a generation's time span, but a four-year-old does not know this, and with his great propensity for learning language, he absorbs this English dialect as a second native tongue. Of course, the influence of television speech cannot be discounted, and Carlo will probably understand spoken, standard English quite well. However, when he must speak English, it is likely that he will only be able to use the neighborhood dialect in which he has had experience as an active speaker. When Carlo turns six and begins to attend public school, he will be confronted with using standard English orally as well as with learning a written representation of standard English, while his teacher will understand almost nothing about his neighborhood dialect and will, at best, be proficient in a standard form of Spanish.

It may well be that transient neighborhood dialects ought not be the object of large-scale, truly scholarly linguistic investigations. Teachers, however, can begin to develop some tentative understandings about the functioning of some major grammatical features of even a neighborhood dialect by organizing the way they listen to youngsters talking to each other when they are at play or in the lunchroom. They can observe how a word is used, its frequency of usage, or how the past is formed, and they can listen to these features for a period of time, excluding all other structural characteristics, until they have achieved some generalizations about the ones in question. They can then extend their observations to other grammatical features. Such systematic listening is likely to produce, albeit slowly, some grammatical understanding of an ethnic group's dialect. What is more, there is every reason to believe that youngsters will benefit from teachers sharing with them the grammatical rules they have discovered about their own neighborhood speech and engaging them in comparing the rules describing standard English with those describing their local dialect. Such comparisons need not be complete to increase youngsters' comprehension of the functioning of morphology, phonology, and syntax, and even extend their insights into the possible variations in meaning that apparently similar forms of speaking can assume.

DENOTATIONS AND CONNOTATIONS

There is a certain level of comprehension between native speakers of diverse English dialects, which tends to dull people's awareness of what they are not understanding. They may think they understand, but do so only partially. They may be offended by a certain turn of speech when no offense was intended. In other words, comparative studies of native English dialects might help not only teachers achieve insights into ethnic differences but students as well, if they were drawn into the endeavor.

In recent years, expressions and unusual vocabulary, derived from numerous dialectal sources, have captured the public's attention. There is, indeed, a fascination and usefulness in learning the denotative (or dictionary) meaning of such expressions as *ace boon coon,* (black dialect for top man or VIP), *playing the dozens* (black dialect for a game-like exchange of insults frequently concerning the participants' mothers), *schlemiel* (Yiddish term for a born loser), and *barrio* (Spanish term used by Mexican Americans to indicate the neighborhood). However, terms such as these often carry with them whole sets of implicit meanings that are neither clearly delineated nor always intended. These connotations may lie close to the surface or they may be brought to the surface by the way they are placed in a sentence, by the context in which they are used, or even by the social role of the person speaking.

The possibility for ethnic miscues is greatest when the dictionary definition of a word is similar but the connotations vary considerably. For example, a word such as stupid in standard English does not have a very positive meaning. This meaning, however, is somewhat mitigated by a connotation of temporary foolishness, which lies close to the surface and allows rather free usage of the word in a semi-joking fashion. A native speaker of standard English might, without too much fear of offending, ask an acquaintance, "How could you do something so stupid?" He might also say of himself, "I am rather stupid about things like this," and mean only that he has not had very much previous experience. On the other hand, for native speakers of Spanish and Italian, the use of the word stupid which closely resembles their own word, *stupido,* arouses feelings of deep indignation and resentment, for in their native tongues it would only be used with the purpose of offending or as a sign of extreme exasperation. Because the phonological and denotative aspects of the word are similar, they often are unaware that they have taken the connotations of the word from their own native languages and superimposed these on the standard English word. The reverse, of course, is just as likely to happen.

These close-to-the-surface connotations are more easily dealt with than those arising from contextual circumstances. For instance, a standard, though informal, English sentence such as, "She is the last of the red, hot mammas," can range in connotations from a singing style reminiscent of the rather hefty, deep-throated Sophie Tucker to "the lady is long past her prime" to "she is sexually aggressive." A non-native speaker of standard English, familiar with the Sophie Tucker allusion, might easily find himself in a socially difficult situation because he described a friend's sister using the "red hot mamma" phrase to indicate her singing aspirations. Rumbles have been started over less.

DISCUSSION MODES

Beyond the more traditional rubrics of language study dealt with above, i.e., syntax, morphology, semantics, and phonology, there is, for teachers, another way of viewing language development that is extremely important to understanding an ethnic group's ways of communicating verbally— that is, the discussion modes employed by a group in its various kinds of discussion. How do people of the same ethnic group engage in discussion when they are among themselves, at parties, at home with their families, or at meetings of committees?

Youngsters bring with them a series of discussion modes when they enter a new kind of situation such as the public education system. In all probability, they have no experience with any kind of public, multi-ethnic situation, and they lack the objectivity necessary to choose speaking styles other than those they learned at home and in their neighborhoods. Children's most natural ways of engaging in discussion and whether these could lead to inter-ethnic misunderstandings, are important instructional information.

If a boy interrupts someone during an interesting, controversial discussion, is that rude in the context of his own heritage or is it a demonstration of commitment or deep interest? Are interruptions strictly a result of his personality or can similar patterns of interruptions be found among other members of the same ethnic group? If a girl seems to talk as though everyone else knows less than she does (without actually using these words), is this a reflection of the styles adopted in discussions at home indicating no more than, "I truly believe what I am saying," or is she an egoist who needs to be dealt with? The girl may not be aware that a discussion mode she uses in the heat of a discussion offends other people in the group.

Educators have ignored the fundamental ethnic differences in the ways youngsters talk to each other even though they have made class discussion one of their major tools of instruction. The discussion mode most easily associated with scholastic ethnicity follows a "you-take-a-turn-then-another-takes-a-turn" model, except when the teacher wants to talk and then it is "everyone-waits-until-I-finish-even-if-I-talk-the-whole-hour" model. Within the context of scholastic ethnicity, everyone speaking at the same time is an anathema. At home though, or out with friends, the one-at-a-time discussion mode often goes by the wayside, especially if people are involved in their discussions. Other posible reasons aside, it behooves teachers to determine the diverse kinds of discussion strategies employed by students of different ethnic backgrounds when they are involved in, say, controversial or inflammatory discussions, creative or flights-of-imagination discussions, and investigative or getting-to-the-bottom-of-things discussions. Such insights may well increase a teacher's ability to orchestrate interesting, productive classroom discussions with a high learning value.

The assumption that the best way to engage in classroom discussion is to follow the "you-take-a-turn-then-another-takes-a-turn" model needs to be reconsidered. For some circumstances and objectives, it may be the best way—but that is a conclusion that remains to be proven. After all, children who are waving their hands frantically to get their turn may not be listening to anyone else. Furthermore, it is doubtful if the kind of involvement that is often achieved in activities outside of school can be achieved in school when only one kind of group discussion pattern is allowed. The kinds of verbal interactions that go on among family and friends are of an ethnic origin belonging to one's heritage. The verbal interactions of scholastic ethnicity often seem *not* to be a part of the "real" world.

The entire problem of discussion modes began to develop in my mind quite by accident. I had invited five black students in an economic opportunity program to my graduate workshop. The ostensible purpose was to discuss the inadequacies of university programs for diverse ethnic minorities. The discussion was, to begin with, quite orderly, that is, first one person spoke, then another, and so forth. However, as the discussion turned to more heated topics, the black Americans literally took it over. The whites in the group (more than half) sat as though they were an audience invited to observe an extraordinary event. The blacks seemed to all talk at once, becoming progressively louder and more shrill in pitch. Even as teacher, I did not feel there was any opportunity for me to interject an opinion or comment. There was a lull, and most unexpectably one of the black girls turned to the whites who were gathered on one side of the circle:

"And you," she asked pointing her finger at them, "why aren't you joining in? Do you think you're too good to tell us how you feel?" The whites seemed to find no way to respond to her accusation, and I, myself, was stunned. Vaguely in my mind I had decided that the black group was determined to take over the discussion and make those "whiteys" listen. There really had been, as far as I could remember, no pause that would have let any of the whites enter the animated discussion. Furthermore, so many people seemed to be talking at once that I had trouble following what was being said.

I had set up two tape recorders thinking that the discussion might be useful in some future class. I went home and listened to those tapes for hours, trying to understand why there had been such a fundamental misunderstanding between the two groups. As I listened, I began to realize that I was hearing a mode of group discussion very different from what I was accustomed to. It was the same kind of feeling I had while living in Italy! In groups Italians always seemed to talk to each other with so much animation and so many people expressed themselves at the same time that I often ceased to follow the discussion. Yet I had always had the feeling that I could take part in the conversation if I wanted. I kept asking myself why my reaction to the black discussion was different. I had a number of tapes made at social gatherings in Italy that I had brought home mostly as souvenirs. I tried to compare these with the tapes I had made recently in class.

The strategy I used was to try to pinpoint when a second, third, fourth, or fifth speaker entered an ongoing discussion. I thought the actual amount of time that passed between one speaker's entry into the discussion and the next speaker's entry might hold the key, but this did not seem to be the case on the tapes I listened to. I did, however, find a relationship in the black discussion mode between the speaker's tonal pitch, the gist of the speech, and the entry of another speaker into the discussion.

Whether the previous speaker had actually finished seemed to be of little importance. As a black speaker reached his or her point, i.e., the real gist of what he or she was saying, his or her voice rose several tones above the initial pitch. Not having the necessary instruments nor the trained ear, I was unable to determine the specific rise in pitch, but within a few moments after a speaker's pitch began to descend, someone else added her or his voice to the discussion. The first speaker continued for various lengths of time to complete his or her point, while the second speaker slowly climbed to a climatic pitch and his or her gist. Once the voice started to settle into a lower pitch range, a third speaker joined, and the process tended to repeat itself. Loudness seemed to be a result of the number of speakers actually expressing themselves. The more speakers, the louder the discussion became. A diagram of the discussion pattern that I discerned follows:

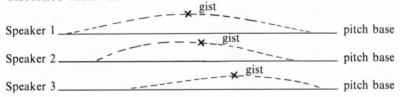

As the diagram indicates, there was no pause in the talking pattern of the discussion. This lack of pauses may have been the reason why the whites present felt excluded from the discussion.

The souvenir tapes I had brought home from Italy revealed a different kind of discussion mode. My Italian friends did all talk at once, but in a fashion quite different from the discussion mode noted on the classroom tapes. Several speakers would begin to talk simultaneously, almost as if they were vying with each other for the spotlight. Exactly how or why I do not know, but one of the speakers would win out and be allowed his or her say. A longer than usual pause in his or her discussion would signal to the others that he or she was nearing the end of what he or she had to say. Sometimes he or she was allowed to finish; sometimes the others would jump in and contend again for the speaker's spot even though the first speaker had not quite finished. A diagram of the discussion pattern that I discerned from my Italian tapes follows:

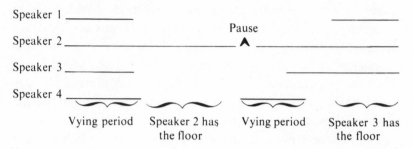

Speaker 1 _____
                                                Pause
Speaker 2 _____ **A** _____

Speaker 3 _____

Speaker 4 _____

Vying period   Speaker 2 has   Vying period   Speaker 3 has
                the floor   the floor

I hypothesized that the pause that appeared frequently before the onset of the vying period might have been unconsciously interpreted by me as an invitation to join in.

A diagram of the typical classroom discussion mode follows for comparative purposes:

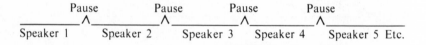

          Pause   Pause   Pause   Pause
_____**A**_____**A**_____**A**_____**A**_____
Speaker 1   Speaker 2   Speaker 3   Speaker 4   Speaker 5 Etc.

While this discussion mode is the one most typically adopted by teachers, it may be that students whose ethnic discussion modes are quite different have trouble relating to a topic that is discussed in ways not normally used among their family and friends. A discussion mode that might prove difficult for a middle-class white youngster to comprehend might be the most comprehensible format for a youngster of another ethnic background.

As a tour escort, I remember American tourists frequently commented with much amazement about how Spaniards or Italians all seemed to be speaking at the same time. I also remembered that most of my tourists had a way of all talking at the same time but in a different way. In recent years, I have begun to explore this thought in relationship to possibly different white ethnicities that might exist in America. In the

Midwest I have observed a discussion mode of all talking at the same time that does seem to differ substantially from any of those described above. It goes something like this: the speaker holding the floor reaches his or her gist, listeners begin to lose interest, which is first signaled by their removing their gaze from the speaker and beginning a whispered conversation with another listener or two; soon there are several small groups of conversation, and the speaker continues what she or he has to say in a small group unit (usually those within direct eye range so that visual contact seems to hold these listeners) and in a reduced voice volume. Soon, a second speaker desiring a larger audience will begin to widen his or her visual eye contact to include listeners from another small group. If the second speaker succeeds in obtaining several listeners outside his or her own group, he or she will raise his or her voice volume and make more use of emphatic pitch tones. A diagram of this process follows.

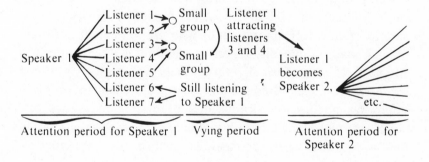

It is quite possible that the differences between the discussion modes of one's ethnic heritage and those of scholastic ethnicity cause school discussions to be labelled irrelevant, even when the topics discussed are of direct concern to the daily lives of students. Certainly some provision could be made to build into lesson plans discussions that could be carried out in several modes, so that members of diverse ethnic groups could feel, once in a while, that they participated in a truly relevant kind of discussion in school.

OUTLINING VERBAL COMMUNICATION

The accompanying outline of verbal communication is an effort not only to describe verbal ethnic traits, but to do so in a way useful to teachers. It would probably look different if the audience or objective were different. The action-oriented purpose of this study has influenced the outline in important ways.

For example, discussion modes, which are included as a subcategory of the verbal aspect of ethnicity, are identified with *qualities of discussion* rather than, as was possible, with the specific social functions of a discussion—that is, instead of greetings, formal introductions, and the like serving as the bases for observations, kinds of discussions such as controversial-inflammatory, informative, investigative, and the like were used. Thus, an ethnic profile would try to describe the patterns of discussion that were used by members of an ethnic group whenever a controversy, or an exchange of information, and the like, were present in a discussion. While the social function of a discussion is an important factor among adults who are competent not only in their own ethnic discussion modes but in the temporary adoption of more formal, more widely understood speaking strategies, young children are almost wholly dependent on their somewhat unconscious knowledge of discussion modes acquired through their ethnic heritage. This is especially true in the lower grades when scholastic ethnicity is just beginning to develop in youngsters. In general, our assumption was that the qualitative aspects of a discussion were more likely to generate the use of ethnically-acquired discussion modes in the classroom than would the social function of a discussion.

We did not expect to achieve a thorough understanding of any one native tongue, unless this had already been achieved by experts in that field. We were more interested in concentrating on characteristics that teachers would encounter or could use in teaching than on a detailed description of a language. Our emphasis was on comparing language and discussion traits of an ethnic origin, which teachers would most frequently have to deal with and which would differ in important ways from the teachers' own native tongue, assumed to be, for our study, standard English. In sum, the outline we devised for verbal communication is horizontal in nature rather than vertical. Comparing linguistic traits across languages is more vital for instructional improvement than in-depth descriptions within a language. The outline reflects this kind of choice.

FOOTNOTES

[1]William Labov, *The Social Stratification of English in New York City* (Washington, D.C.: Center for Applied Linguistics, 1966).

[2]Among such studies are: Donald Lloyd, "Subcultural Patterns Which Affect Language and Reading Development," in *Improving English Skills of Culturally Different Youth* Washington, D.C.: U.S.O.E. and Paul Lauther, "The Short Happy Life of Adams-Morgan Community School Project," *Harvard Educational Review,* Vol. 38, No. 2, Spring 1968, pp. 235-262.

[3]Martin Deutsch, "The Disadvantaged Child and the Learning Process," in *Education in Depressed Areas,* A. Harry Passow, ed. (New York: Teachers College Press, 1963) p. 174.

[4]William Labov, *Language in the Inner City; Studies in the Black English Vernacular* (Philadelphia: University of Pennsylvania Press, 1972), Chapter 5, "The Logic of Nonstandard English."

VERBAL COMMUNICATION

A. Categories describing oral language
   1. Grammatical structure
      a. Syntax
      b. Morphology
   2. Semantic
      a. Denotative
      b. Connotative
   3. Phonological
      a. Sound formation
      b. Pausal behavior
      c. Tempo
      d. Rhythm
      e. Pitch range
      f. Others

B. Ethnic criteria for judging verbal communication with regard to socio-economic status, intellectual capacity, sociability, etc.:
   1. Use of speech evaluation rules
   2. Selection and use of discussion modes
   3. Others

C. Discussion modes according to the kind of discussion
   1. Informative
   2. Controversial
   3. Exploratory-inquiry
   4. Playful
   5. Insulting
   6. Others

Using the above outline, comparative studies may be undertaken, as per the following model:

Native Language 1	*Standard English*	*Native Language 2*
(Language learned during ethnic period of learning after language of heritage has been acquired)	(Assumed to be either native language 1 or native language 2 of teacher)	(Language learned during first stages of language development as a result of the immediate environment)

CHAPTER V

Nonverbal Communciation

Each one of us possesses a system of facial expression, body movements, and spatial arrangements that communicate meaning to others. The way we look at people, our gestures, even the way we touch, are forms of nonverbal communication by means of which we say things about ourselves to others and from which others receive impressions about us. For example, two strangers sitting opposite each other in an empty subway car with nothing else to do but look at each other avert their eyes and try to paint blank expressions on their faces. They are saying to each other, "I respect your privacy." On a very crowded subway with riders squeezed tightly together, a woman usually knows whether she is being touched because of the crowded conditions or because some man is making a pass. Two people immersed in conversation will continually nod their heads as a sign that they are listening attentively.

People, often quite unconsciously, do things with their bodies that are sufficiently systematic to carry meaning. Along with one's native tongue, there is a powerful system of nonverbal communication that one begins to learn almost from birth. As in language acquisition, children, capable of a vast number of movements, concentrate on a relatively few. They learn a non-verbal language system, called by Birdwhistell a *diakinesic system.*[1] If the communicants are of the same ethnic group, they are likely to use the same diakinesic system much as they are likely to use the same verbal dialect. In a sense, a diakinesic system is a nonverbal dialect, which may be absorbed much the way a native tongue is acquired in early childhood. We are, however, a good deal more aware of our verbal forms of communication than of our nonverbal, perhaps because speech, through reading and writing, has been repeatedly acknowledged in a formalized way. With the advent of motion pictures and television, a similar phenomenon may now be happening to nonverbal communication.

Differences in nonverbal communication systems may very well be a major cause of the dislike and distrust that ethnic groups sometimes feel for each other. They perceive meaning from the movements and spatial arrangements of others through their own diakinesic and spatial systems, attributing to certain gestures and arrangements meanings that were not intended. All this may occur at a low or even no level of awareness so that there is a feeling of being uncomfortable without really knowing why. If someone stands too close, such a feeling may arise. I personally recall eating at a hot dog stand and becoming exceedingly apprehensive about a gentleman who kept staring at me. He never did anything but study me unabashedly, yet I was wary and untrusting of him. As it turned out, the counter girl with whom I spoke after he left told me he was from Italy. I then remembered how I had been struck by the way people in Italy would just stop and stare at others on the street. Once my car broke down in Rome, and not only did several Italians offer to help me, but a huge crowd gathered to watch. They obviously felt it was perfectly proper to stop and watch whatever might catch their curiosity on a street.

Birdwhistell's observational study of smiling behaviors in the United States reveals regional differences of considerable significance. He found that the frequency of smiling varied from section to section:

> Middle-class individuals from Ohio, Indiana, and Illinois, as counted on the street, smiled more often than did New Englanders with a comparable background from Massachusetts,

New Hampshire, and Maine. Moreover these latter subjects smiled with a higher frequency than did Western New Yorkers. At the other extreme, the highest incidence of smiling was observed in Atlanta, Louisville, Memphis, and Nashville.[2]

Birdwhistell's investigation also reveals that the meaning attached to smiling behavior seems to vary regionally:

In one part of the country, an unsmiling individual might be queried as to whether he was "angry about something," while in another, the smiling individual might be asked, "what's funny?" In one area, an apology required an accompanying smile; in another, the smile elicited the response that the apology was not "serious."[3]

That the smile may be an innate human action is not debated by Birdwhistell. His point is that children learn the appropriate situations for this behavior and subordinate smiling to the contexts so that a socially comprehensible meaning is achieved. In other words, children become competent in a set of strategies for nonverbal communication during the ethnic stages of their development.

People of different ethnic groups are probably unaware of the diversities of meanings that may exist in otherwise quite similar nonverbal expressions. Ethnocentric preconceptions are especially powerful when people are unaware such preconceptions, as is still the case with nonverbal forms of communication. Certainly, for teaching situations, where persons of different ethnic backgrounds are continually interacting, an increased awareness of diakinesic systems holds promise for improving interpersonal relationships. While teaching in Gary, I might have mistaken a young man's apology as being insincere because he smiled, when actually he meant to convey that the behavior would not happen again. From my perspective, smiling means, at the least, feeling good, whereas I would expect someone who was really sorry *not* to feel good, and not to smile. I tend to react very negatively to a student I think is "putting me on." Not only might such a reaction be a real injustice, but the youngster might decide that I "have it in for him" and perceive of my class as a time to "make war," thereby beginning that vicious cycle in which classroom control becomes central and learning becomes the product of threats.

KINESICS

There seem to be several interlocking nonverbal systems operating simultaneously, which is also true in verbal communication. Studies in nonverbal communication have taken several directions. *Kinesics,* which is the scientific study of communication based on the body's motions, is at the initial stages of development. Ray L. Birdwhistell has devised a notational system with which to record body movements. The symbols or kinegraphs are classified according to movements in eight sections of the body: *1)* total head, *2)* face, *3)* trunk, *4)* shoulder, arm, and wrist, *5)* hand and finger activity, *6)* hip, leg, and ankle, *7)* foot activity, walking, and *8)* neck.[4] While the notational system is fairly complex and not easily used by teachers, some possible adaptations to school usage will be suggested further on.

The forms of analysis developed by Birdwhistell have their roots in the research techniques of the structural and descriptive grammarians.[5] The minimal body movement carrying significance is called a kineme and is comparable to a phoneme in oral language and a grapheme in written language. There are different uses for body communication. The movement may carry a clear denotative or even connotative meaning independent of what is being said verbally; it may also act as a punctuation system for the spoken language, giving emphasis, or drama, or rhythm to a speaker's works. Although a speaker may not be conscious of her or his movements, they are not haphazard but, rather, fit into predictable patterns.

Birdwhistell is attempting to design a kinemic catalog of the American diakinesic system. Of the approximately 20,000 facial expressions physiologically possible, 32 kinemes in the face and head area have been observed.[6] In the light of the large number of possible movements, it is reasonable to suppose that the kinemic catalog of other nationalities as well as of ethnic groups of one nationality will be comprised of different sets of kinemes. If a sufficient number of catalogs and accompanying kinesic meanings can be developed, a great step toward inter-ethnic understanding and a pluralistic society could be achieved.

Present research is still in the initial stages of describing one diakinesic system in all its varied functions. Oral languages have long been the object of such study, and numerous linguistic systems have been amply described so that what sentences will look or sound like can be predicted for many languages. Nonverbal studies have not reached such levels of empirical knowledge. Because simple objective descriptions of what is going on in a diakinesic system have not yet been worked out, it is difficult to move to the more complex level of trying to determine what associations might exist in people's mind between socio-economic status, intellectual capacity, and so on, and certain kinemes. Such associations do seem to exist; each of us seems to carry around a set of criteria by which we judge people beyond the meanings we receive from their nonverbal actions.

An older woman sitting with her knees at angles away from each other gives a low socioeconomic impression of herself even if she is wearing slacks. This was, at least, the result I obtained by showing photographs of the same woman, dressed in the same clothes but seated in different positions, to 143 teachers and future teachers living in the Detroit area. Each teacher saw only one photograph and was asked to quickly imagine what kind of work the woman might do. In no case, did they think the photo of the woman with her knees angled apart was of a teacher. Suggestions varied widely from housewife to saleswoman to dog catcher. When the photo of the woman with legs were crossed was shown, approximately 42 per cent of those viewing it thought she might be a teacher or school administrator. Some thought she might be a salesperson in a dress shop.

Notwithstanding our present lack of knowledge regarding diakinesic systems and how they convey meaning and the even more obscure way in which our judgments about diakinesic systems operate, teachers are constantly involved in making classroom decisions based on nonverbal communication. This means that even though the average teacher cannot hope to achieve an in-depth understanding of any one diakinesic system, she or he must begin to study those nonverbal characteristics that most seem to disturb or please or in some way give impressions relevant to her or his teaching. Teachers must begin to explore what specific meanings they derive from a behavior and how their *own* nonverbal behavior might differ when communicating the same meaning. They can force themselves to analyze judgments they are making about students to determine what aspects of those judgments are based on nonverbal information. Furthermore, if a number of the same ethnic group are present in the school, a teacher could draw up a list of nonverbal descriptions relevant to the group and ask other teachers in the school to determine whether they have made similar observations "frequently," "sometimes," or "not at all." Interpretations of these nonverbal behaviors can be explored with other teachers not merely to ascertain agreement but real differences, which is a means for teachers to explore some of their own ethnic traits and to determine where these might be leading to unfortunate inter-ethnic miscues.

PROXEMICS

Studies in nonverbal communication also include the systems of spatial arrangements that people use continually in their daily contacts. The study of interpersonal space, or *proxemics,* has been pursued by Edward T. Hall, [7] who has noted the consistent differences in the arrangement of interpersonal space that can be observed from nation to nation—the sense of crowding that North Americans have in Latin American countries and the feeling of distance and aloofness they have in England or Scandinavia.

Personality as well as cultural differences also seem to operate in the arrangement of interpersonal space. The results, for example, of John L. Williams' investigations have indicated that introverts keep a greater distance from other people than do extroverts.[8] It is also probable that sharing certain feelings such as fear tends to reduce spatial distances between people.[9] Notwithstanding such considerations, it has long been recognized among playwrights and creative artists what the works of Hall have underscored—there are patterns of interpersonal spatial relationships typifying cultural (and, for this author, more specifically ethnic) groups.

A number of ethnic differences in spatial arrangements within the classroom context have been described by Robert Sommer. Sommer notes, for example, the discomfit that English-Canadian teachers may feel among French-Canadian students who seem to be invading their space by coming closer to them than would be customary for members of their own group.[10] Since English Canadians are probably not aware of their own ethnic traits with regard to space, a feeling of being assaulted or somehow affronted may arise. Sommer also discusses the close spatial contacts that typify Jewish children of New York's Lower East Side and Puerto Rican Americans, suggesting (though not advocating) that teachers from other backgrounds might be prepared for this different usage of space.[11]

With reference to classroom spatial arrangements, Sommer notes that, "The teacher has 50 times more free space than the students with the mobility to move about."[12] What meaning students attach to such spatial arrangements is not really clear. Whether such meanings derive from their own ethnic heritages and are unwittingly applied to a different ethnic situation, that of the school, remains an uninvestigated question. Sommer does not consider the question and instead cites descriptions of typical spatial arrangements in schools by writers of vastly different ethnic heritages (e.g., Jonathan Swift and Maria Montessori) and transfers these to American schools, implying, in the final analysis, that scholastic spatial arrangements carry the same meaning of teacher domination and student restriction for a number of nationalities.

There is the possibility that scholastic ethnicity makes the spatial arrangements between teachers and students not only less offensive, but capable of carrying meaning other than that of authority and restriction. For instance, it might very well indicate to students that the teacher is there for all of them. Since each student is able to clearly view the teacher, there is a sense of equality among students. The truth of either of these meanings is, of course, questionable, for the variations in meanings produced by ethnic differences remain to be investigated and, hopefully, mapped in some systematic fashion.

Put in everyday terms, if I approach you and you back away from me, what meanings might I attach to this spatial arrangement? Will such meanings remain unchanged, given a similar context, from ethnic group to ethnic group? If we stand close to each other but side by side does that carry a different meaning than if we stand close together but facing each other squarely? What differences in meaning might arise from ethnic diversities? What are the spatial conflicts that might arise between scholastic ethnicity and the ethnicities present in America's pluralistic society?

INSTRUMENTS FOR EXPLORING NONVERBAL COMMUNICATION

Motion pictures, videotaping, the slow motion camera, and still photography offer ways of divulging the elements of nonverbal communication more efficiently than teachers' direct observations. However, their expense, the need of getting help from others, and working out photography methods that are unobtrusive in the classroom have inhibited their widespread use. Nevertheless, their ability to obtain objective descriptions of nonverbal communication systems makes them attractive instruments for action researchers. Anthropologist John Collier, Jr., has successfully used still photographs for his studies of nonverbal communication: "In the dynamics of micro-culture, the details of person-to-person relationships can be analyzed through the use of still pictures. Photographs allow for the observation of personal physical bearing, posture, facial expressions, arm and hand gestures."[13] He further notes that photographs can be useful in observing the spatial relationships of gatherings, their cluster patterns, and the possible implications of these for such important social phenomena as leadership.

Motion pictures, videotaping, and the slow motion camera make it possible to follow nonverbal, interpersonal relationships over an extended period of time. Body movements as well as the spatial arrangements between people can be closely reviewed as they are happening. In particular, the synchronization of movements and spatial management between people can be analyzed. Work of this sort has been carried out by the anthropologist Frederick Erickson. One of Erickson's studies involved the repeated videotaping of a job interview situation in which the setting, the job, and the interviewer were all the same; only the applicants changed. At the end of each taping, Erickson had the interviewer and the applicant view the play-back separately. Whenever the viewer felt that the action was significant and he could recall his feelings, he would stop the tape and his comments were recorded. The tapes were analyzed by Erickson for the quality of nonverbal synchronization or lack of it that could be visually observed during the interview. This analysis was compared to the reactions of the subjects during the play-back so that a reasonably accurate picture of the conscious meaning attached to each subject's body movements by the other and by himself was obtained.[14]

Erickson encountered several instances of inadequate nonverbal comprehension between the interviewer and applicant. One applicant of second-generation Italian-American background was visibly disoriented by the frequency with which the interviewer averted his eyes from direct eye contact. During the play-back, the applicant commented several times at the lack of interest in what he was saying as displayed by the interviewer every time he averted his eyes from the applicant. The interviewer, whose background was German-American going back several generations, noted how nervous the applicant seemed to be and how he had tried to put him at ease by looking away (probably so as not to stare or examine him visually for too long a period).

Notwithstanding the obvious advantages of these visual media, the groups I have worked with have never had the means to carry out nonverbal communication studies other than through direct classroom observations, the use of still photography, the study of comic strips, and the responses to various kinds of questionnaires devised to obtain insights into the preferred spatial arrangements of people engaged in specific activities such as studying or competing. A nonverbal observation checklist designed for classroom situations was piloted with some limited success. It is by no means as reliable an instrument as those used by Erickson, but it is better suited to the action research situation in which regularly employed teachers are engaged in objective data collection. A discussion of the instrument and how it was piloted can be found in Appendix A.

HAPTICS

There are forms of nonverbal communication that do not lend themselves easily to visual observation. In particular, in the study of interpersonal touching, or *haptics,* collecting truly objective data is unfeasible, which may explain why this area of nonverbal communication has received so little serious attention. The question of touching is not simply whether people do or do not touch each other but also involves the different qualities of touching and the variations of meanings that such differences connote.

We often hear said that a firm handshake makes a good impression. What if the firm handshake is clammy as well? For a middle-class, white person with a Northeastern U.S.A. background, being held by any part of the arm while being addressed by a business associate would probably prove annoying, confusing, and even threatening. However, if a couple in love, having this same background, are talking, even though not romantically, it is common for the man to hold the woman's hand, rub her arm, or put his arm around her shoulder. Touching, in this case, becomes a sign of continuing affection undiverted by other interests.

I recall a black girl discussing the way white teachers touched her. The girl felt that her teachers did a lot of touching, but it was "mamby pamby" and over-soft rather than pleasantly firm. I was a little embarrassed as I listened to her because I recognized that I often touched my students' backs in a light circular or patting fashion as a way of saying I was fond of them. Again, there is a lack of understanding of the nature of meanings transmitted by touching. However, a vital step in increasing the understanding of nonverbal communication systems is to be consciously aware of the meaningful nature of a touch and of the diverse interpretations possible due to diverse ethnicities.

SYMBOLS AND SIGNALS

Nonverbal communication also includes ways of communicating that are not directly dependent upon the actual presence of others, although the implied presence of two or more people interacting is always there. Both symbols and signals are of this nature. Symbols, in particular, tend to be the result of traditional meanings summed up in nonverbal images. The flag of the United States is more than a representation of the nation; it simultaneously connotes loyalty, pride in country, gratefulness for the bounty of America, and the like. To trample on it has, for many, the significance of trampling on all these meanings. Obviously, individuals learn the meanings underlying symbols from others, but once such symbols are learned and understood, the presence of others is unnecessary.

The age at which the meanings of a symbol are learned is important. If, for example, the flag is respectfully and lovingly treated over and over again while children are still in the pre-abstract stages of development, their adult reactions to the flag are likely to be at a nonlogical but deeply emotional level. Even if they come to criticize allegiance to a piece of cloth, they will probably own up to a "twinge at the heart strings" at seeing a flag unfurled against a blue sky.

Symbols are not necessarily understood by all groups in the same fashion though. Thus, youngsters brought up in the rural Midwest may be sincerely reverent toward the flag, while youngsters brought up in Chicago's inner city may be deeply and ethnically cynical. Can the American flag signify "gratefulness for the bounty of America" to African Americans? Does the recently migrated Mexican American perceive of "pride in country" in the same way as long-arrived Midwesterners? Most of all, can the feelings that are communicated to their children long before the age of abstract reasoning be qualitatively similar? There seems to be ample evidence that such is not the case. To burn a small American flag in a philosophy class has been considered grounds sufficient for a teacher's dismissal, even though the act was part of a scholarly investigation of symbols.[15]

The ethnically based reactions to symbols has remained largely uninvestigated. Minority groups may attribute importance to symbols that have no meaning to outsiders and that may easily be misinterpreted and even misused by nonmembers. While the school imposes a knowledge of its own symbols, little consideration is given to the symbols of others. There is rarely even the effort to talk about the significant symbols of diverse ethnic groups. Yet, symbols often carry combinations of meanings and feelings that are unique to a group.

Again, it is important to make a distinction between symbols experienced during the ethnic stages of development and symbols consciously adopted by a group to exclude other groups. In this latter instance, adults undertake a rational, purposeful action over which they usually exercise complete emotional control. The children of these adults will experience these symbols as ethnic acquisitions and, if their parents are very reverent toward a symbol repeatedly during their childhood, they will, as adults, probably always sense that reverence, even if their own logic has brought them to disavow the symbols in question. This seems to be what has happened to many Americans in their attitudes toward the American flag.

Signals communicate discrete meanings that may be used in isolation from other forms of nonverbal communication. Discrete meanings (denotations) based on body movements are usually incorporated into the diakinesic system and probably comprise most of the denotative meanings expressed by this system. Signals are not part of a nonverbal diakinesic system. Body movements done in isolation from other movement can, however, be classified as signals. For the most part, though, signals have very precise meanings and are intended to communicate with the public at large. Traffic signals are of this nature.

Signals used to communicate with the population as a whole tend to be of broadly cultural rather than of ethnic origin. These signals are usually experienced by youngsters rather late in childhood with a fair amount of infrequency and a good deal of logical explanation from adults. Some signals, such as traffic lights, are usually experienced very early and often with little logical explanation. When a little girl runs across the street against the light, her mother grabs her rudely, loudly reprimanding her for having disobeyed the light, even though no cars were coming in either direction. Despite such instances, signals will probably hold only peripheral importance for the classroom teacher.

OUTLINING NONVERBAL COMMUNICATION

The outline of nonverbal communication is similar in format to that of verbal communication. It is based on describing and comparing the systems followed by members of an ethnic group with those followed by teachers. Since far too little is known about nonverbal communication systems, no "standards" were assumed. It was, nevertheless, felt that to understand nonverbal miscues that are ethnic in origin, teachers have to first understand the meanings they associate with their own nonverbal systems. Furthermore, they have to explore the effects the nonverbal activity of their students have on their impressions of their intellectual capacity, socioeconomic status, and other traits. The criteria used to make such impressionistic judgments may have been absorbed during the pre-abstract stages of teachers' development without the benefit of evidence or rational analysis. Students' responses are equally important: What impressions do teachers' nonverbal behaviors make on their students? Are they interpreting their nonverbal behavior accurately? Comparative mapping will encourage the study of a small number of nonverbal traits exhibited by the members of one ethnic group in such a way that these traits may be compared with those exhibited by another ethnic group in a similar situation.

FOOTNOTES

[1] Ray L. Birdwhistell, *Kinesics and Context* (Philadelphia: University of Pennsylvania Press, 1970) p. 17.

[2] Ibid., p. 30.

[3] Ibid., p. 31.

[4] Ibid., p. 258.

[5] Ibid., p. XIII.

[6] Ibid., pp. 99-100.

[7] Edward T. Hall, *The Silent Language* (New York: Doubleday, 1959), and *The Hidden Dimensions* (New York: Doubleday, 1966).

[8] John L. Williams, "Personal Space and Its Relationship to Extroversion-Introversion" (Master's Thesis, University of Alberta, 1963).

[9] S. Feshback and N. Feshback, "Influence of the Stimulus Object upon the Complementary and Supplementary Projection of Fear," *Journal of Abnormal and Social Psychology,* LXVI, 1963, pp. 498-502.

[10] Robert Sommer, *Personal Space: The Behavioral Basis of Design* (Englewood Cliffs: Prentice Hall, 1969) p. 27.

[11] Ibid.

[12] Ibid., p. 99.

[13] John Collier, Jr., *Visual Anthropology: Photography as a Research Method* (New York: Holt, Rinehart and Winston, 1967) p. 39.

[14] Frederick Erickson, Presentation at The College of Education, University of Illinois, 1971.

[15] Such an instance of firing actually occurred at Indiana State University in the late sixties.

NONVERBAL COMMUNICATION

A. Diakinesic System
   1. Semantic (meanings independent of verbal)
      a. Denotative
      b. Connotative
   2. Punctuational (used primarily to accompany verbal)
   3. Other

B. Proxemics System
   1. Distances held during various kinds of interaction
   2. Command of availability of space
   3. Spatial arrangements of people, furniture, etc.
   4. Other

C. Haptics (Touching)
   1. Frequency of touch
   2. Quality of touch
   3. Location of touch
   4. Other

D. Symbols

E. Signals

Using the above outline, comparative studies may be undertaken per the following model:

Ethnic Systems of Nonverbal Communication I (belonging to a student or group of students in a school)	*Ethnic Systems of Nonverbal Communication I* (belonging to a teacher or group of teachers in a school)

Note: Possibility of Comparing Scholastic Nonverbal System with Those of Ethnic Heritage

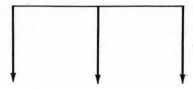

CHAPTER VI

Orientation Modes

In the course of our many observations in schools, I became increasingly aware that much of the nonverbal exchange we were observing was not really a part of any communication system. Students would be sitting alone at large tables in a high school library, reading or doing their homework and without any intention of communicating with others. Nevertheless, there were certain predictable ways they would sit or arrange their books. If they were thinking about how to phrase a sentence, for instance, they would raise their heads, turn their eyes upward, perhaps chew on a pen, and, then, after a few seconds return to their usual writing positions. These nonverbal activities were probably learned at some very early stage to be proper ways of behaving in a library, but their use, regardless of the presence of others, seemed to indicate an aspect of ethnicity that, though nonverbal, was not communication, at least not in the sense of two or more people exchanging messages.

Of course, one can be said to be communicating with oneself. This, however, cannot be seen as an *inter*active ethnic activity but rather as an activity not needing the presence of others, that is, *intra*active and dependent upon the kinds of behaviors that an individual requires of and for himself or herself. These personal requirements, molded by one's ethnic group, I call orientation modes. These patterns of behavior, used regardless of the presence of others, are ways of orienting oneself to the differing contexts of one's usual environment.

BODY ORIENTATIONS

Leaving such a public place as a school library and going into the home, the concept of orientation modes may become a little clearer. Let's suppose one is watching television and no one else is at home. We are completely relaxed, and there can be no intention of communicating with anyone. Nevertheless, there are certain sitting positions we are very likely to assume while other positions are highly unlikely. This realization was first derived from a book I read entitled *Nonverbal Communication in Human Interaction.*[1] It contains a chart of the different positions people of different nationalities predictably take while standing and relaxing, sitting, eating, and so on. One position for relaxation while standing that is practiced by natives of the Sudan, Venezuela, and elsewhere is to stand on one leg while resting the sole of the other foot on the side of the knee of the supporting leg. The knee of the nonsupporting leg is directed, at almost right angles, away from the supporting leg. It is a position that I would not assume even in my wildest dreams, let alone for any form of relaxation.[2]

While Knapp was talking about sets of predictable body positions different national groups display, I became increasingly convinced that ethnic groups were likely to have similarly predictable diversities in the positions their bodies take even when communication is not intended. Given the numerous studies in nonverbal communication that indicate the existence of learned diakinesic systems, it seems most conceivable to me that non-verbal behaviors initiated by usual environments but without the intent of communication would also be influenced by the immediate ethnic group. In all probability, orientation modes, like nonverbal communication, are learned forms of behavior that, by adulthood, become so much a part of our ways of acting that we continue doing them regardless of whether anyone is present. For example, when children first begin to do homework, they adapt their approach to studying according to the circumstances of their home. If parents insist that there be quiet and orderliness when they study, they will come to need such conditions whenever they study. On the other hand, the conditions to which I adapted when I first started studying at home were quite different. I grew up doing my homework while watching television. I doubt that this was the most efficient way to do homework, but it is what I grew accustomed to as a child. I actually did not realize how significant television was for my study habits until I came to writing my doctoral dissertation. I had a very quiet room with a good typewriter and plenty of space to spread my papers around. Notwithstanding, I found I worked ineffectively in quiet with the lack of visual stimulation. I finally had to write my dissertation in a busy reading room at the Indiana University library. Furthermore, to this day, I cannot watch television without doing something else such as reading a newspaper. Yet I have older friends with central Illinois and Indiana backgrounds of several generations standing, who not only give their undivided attention to television but are actually disturbed by my reading if we happen to be watching a television program together.

Orientation modes can be and have been observed in the schools. For instance, Sommer compared the sitting behavior of students in a college library and in a college cafeteria, noting:

> The presence of six (library) chairs on each side of the table guaranteed that no more than twelve individuals would occupy the table, even though there was space for several others. If a student were so inclined, he could have pulled up an additional chair. Moving chairs was a common practice in the college cafeteria both during mealtime and nonmeal hours when it was used as a study hall and lounge.[3]

Sommer seems to assume that some form of communication is occurring. I tend to believe that the unwillingness to move chairs in a library has more to do with our attitudes toward studying and the behaviors we have learned that mean study as opposed to lounging. Psychologists might refer to this as a psychological set, and I would certainly not disagree. I would, however, go a step beyond and call it an ethnic mind set or orientation mode as well.

At this point, I must again acknowledge the difficulty in clearly distinguishing between individual traits and ethnic traits. Personality differences do not negate ethnic differences; there is, in all probability, an interaction between ethnic traits and unique personality traits, which tends to simultaneously affirm our membership in an ethnic group and our individuality as an entity in its own right. To turn to a simpler context, the rules of a specific language are learned and followed by all the members of a group. Some members will use rich, fanciful vocabulary, perhaps even invent words, while others will be very succinct and functional in their choice of vocabulary; all will still be using the same language rules. In a similar fashion, members of certain ethnic groups acquire some basic characteristics for studying, such as needing quiet, without, however, modifying other traits that remain individual choice, such as being able and interested in memorizing historical dates or having special capabilities for solving quantitative problems.

Of course, the importance an ethnic group may give to one or another kind of individual trait may turn it into an ethnic one. If a group happens to give great importance to mathematics, more members of that group are likely to emphasize their mathematical capabilities than would be the case among ethnic groups not having such an emphasis. Thus, we often say the Germans are very mathematical or that the Japanese have a special knack for making electronic products.

ATTENTION MODES

Had it been only the diversity of body positions different ethnic groups may assume under similar environmental circumstances, the development of an orientation category in our scheme might have been unwarranted, but the realization that

ethnic mind sets are present when one studies, plus another related realization, made my students and me feel a new category
was necessary.

At the time, I was conducting a teacher-training project in
twelve Chicago inner-city schools. In one of the junior high
schools there was a large Spanish-speaking population, and it
was not unusual to find two-thirds and even three-fourths of a
class comprised of native Spanish-speaking youngsters. Although we were mindful of the very real ethnic differences between Cuban Americans, Puerto Rican Americans, and Mexican Americans, the school was either unaware of such differences or unwilling to divulge them to outsiders. Most of the
information we had about the students' backgrounds came
either from their teachers or the youngsters themselves. Puerto
Rican Americans and Mexican Americans seemed to be equally
present in the school, while there were very few Cuban Americans.

One English teacher was especially helpful and very willing to
receive whatever insights she could from our investigations. She
even asked us for help. In particular, she was very concerned
about a class that was supposed to be studying Shakespeare's
Julius Caesar. About half her students were third-or fourth-gen-
eration Irish or Polish Americans, largely from middle-class or
blue-collar socioeconomic circumstances. The others were first-
generation, Spanish-speaking Americans whose socioeconomic
backgrounds were somewhat less affluent, judging from their
less expensive clothing.

She had found teaching *Julius Caesar* in this class a near impossible undertaking. No sooner would she begin to discuss a
scene than one of the Spanish-speaking students would interrupt with some apparently unrelated observation. It was all
done good naturedly, and the teacher not only liked but really
enjoyed the Spanish-speaking youngsters. She found, however,
that she could never complete a lesson plan and that the con-
stant interruptions were interfering with other students who,
though not eager, were willing to learn something about
Shakespeare.

She brought into class a cardboard replica of an Elizabethan stage and placed it, semi-permanently, in the middle of her own desk. The interest in the replica seemed very high, and, at first, the many interrupting references to the model, made while she was trying to introduce the play, were taken by her to indicate curiosity about the model. She decided to drop the introduction and talk about the unusual features of the Elizabethan stage. For a short time, the attention of all the students was high. Just when she was beginning to taste success, one of the Spanish-speaking boys saw a bird outside the window that seemed to resemble one they had been studying the day before. He jumped up, announced his find with great satisfaction at his own ability to recognize the bird, and attracted the attention of most of the Spanish-speaking students. The remaining youngsters tried to ignore the disturbance, and within a few seconds several of the Spanish-speaking youngsters were "sh-shing" each other and making exaggerated efforts at being attentive. The poor English teacher had already lost her train of thought but managed to get back on the track. Within minutes there was another reason for an interruption, this time from a very pleasant Chicano girl who enjoyed taking care of her younger brother (only nine months her junior and a member of the same class) and found he was not paying enough attention to the teacher.

By the end of the class period, the teacher was on the verge of imposing some form of marshall law. Because she really did not want to do anything of the kind, she asked us to observe the class and to see if we could come up with any ideas for maintaining the attention of the Spanish-speaking youngsters. By the age of thirteen and fourteen, she thought, they would certainly have an attention span capacity of at least thirty minutes. The problem was to help them achieve that span. (Whether the study of a Shakespearian play should be imposed on young teenagers was not a choice open to this English teacher.)

For the next four sessions, several of my students and I observed the class in an effort to answer three questions: *1)* Could any pattern in the content of the interruptions be discerned? *2)* Could any regularity with regard to the timing of the interruptions be discerned? *3)* Could the interruptions be attributed to just a few of the Spanish-speaking youngsters or was the phenomenon observable in most of them? While the time for observation and the number of students observed were too limited to make any results more than tentative conclusions, we did come up with a few hypotheses that helped us to develop a successful classroom solution.

We found that the frequency of the interruptions by the Spanish-speaking students did seem to follow a pattern. Somewhere in the neighborhood of three and a half to five minutes, one of the Spanish-speaking youngsters would initiate an interruption. Of the sixteen in the class, five seemed to do most of the initiating. Of these five, four were of Puerto Rican background, which, of course, might have just been a coincidence; with such small numbers, few generalizations beyond that classroom can be made. In any case, we also believed that we had observed an increased readiness among the other Spanish-speaking students to interrupt. After about four minutes of attention, their eyes would wander out the window or they would begin noticeably to fidget in their seats and start to eye each other. When the interruption came, they were all ready to participate. The subjects chosen for interruptions seemed to follow no particular pattern and generally did not hold their attention any better than *Julius Caesar* had succeeded in doing. Indeed, within a minute, they were ready to return to their concentration on Shakespeare.

We realized that the analysis of our observations could have led us to believe that the students were rebelling against the study of Shakespeare or that they did not like the teacher very well and were in some sort of conspiracy to undermine whatever she did in class. We assumed, instead, that they were willing to be in school and had no particular grudge against what they were studying or their teacher. These and similar assumptions led us to examine the nature of their attention spans. Psychologists usually relate the length of a child's attention to biological age, and we certainly could not argue with this. It occurred to us, however, that the similarity in length of attention span at different developmental stages was being taken as an indication that children all pay attention in the same way and that the quality of how they pay attention is not influenced by the diversity of their ethnic backgrounds. I recounted the way I read and watch television and pointed out that I had several friends from New York who were accustomed to doing the same thing.

We reasoned that if there were ethnically formed styles for paying attention, then we were observing the style of paying attention exhibited by the Spanish-speaking students in the class. We accepted as a given that these youngsters could concentrate on a topic for thirty minutes but that they needed diversions from the topic about once every four to five minutes. The question then was how to incorporate in the lesson plan this need for diversion while still respecting the different attention style exhibited by the other students and the teacher. We devised two kinds of lesson plans that we thought might be alternated with the kind usually used by the teacher, which consisted of dealing, as thoroughly as possible, with one or two ideas before proceeding to the next idea. For example, in the original lesson plans the teacher was to work with the Elizabethan stage for one class hour, with Elizabethan history for two hours, and with reading the most important scenes of the play for five class hours. We suggested that these same areas could be covered in the allotted time but instead of completing each topic before going on to the next, class periods could be planned so that the theater, the history, and the play would be dealt with in five-minute segments, alternated with the other areas and thereby serving as diversions for each other. A discussion of the Elizabethan balcony could comprise one five-minute segment; turning to parts of the play that might have made use of a balcony could comprise a second five-minute segment as well as a diversion from the discussion of the balcony. A third segment could be built around the Elizabethan audience, which was comprised of rich and poor, mannered and ill-mannered, endowed and unendowed. Again, the play could be referred to for examples of the kinds of characters that might have been in Shakespeare's audience and that turn up as grave diggers, servants, and the like in his plays. A return to the description of the Elizabethan stage could comprise another five-minute segment, and the reading aloud of several pages of the play might end the lesson plan. This pattern of planned diversion could be repeated for a week so that, in the end, the Elizabethan theater, the Shakespearean play, and Elizabethan history would receive as much attention as in the more linear lesson plan.

We also suggested maintaining the more linear lesson plan but arranging for a series of relevant diversions that would keep the students' minds from wandering. We suggested, for instance, having the youngsters look outside the window at an apartment house built in the 1930s, which in some ways resembled the seating arrangement of an Elizabethan theater, then returning to the topic for approximately five minutes and then using another planned interruption, such as having several students read the same lines in the play to see how many different ways they could be said. The teacher preferred our suggestions based on planned diversions, and we did help her plan a two-week unit, which, in this instance, was very successful.

Much more important than whether we successfully resolved this particular teacher's problem was our realization that ethnicity could significantly influence the way people pay attention as well as the way they study. The public schools have tended to ignore such possibly crucial differences and have continued to reflect in classroom arrangements their own scholastic ethnicity.

SPATIAL-ARCHITECTURAL ORIENTATIONS

In recent times, in an effort to make schools more flexible, school furniture has been given some attention, and movable tables and chairs have replaced the traditional, bolted-down desks and folding seats. In many schools this has produced a continual scattering of tables and chairs in helter skelter fashion and a reversal of the traditional arrangement of furniture. For a number of youngsters attending these schools, such a scattering of furniture may be more compatible with the habits acquired at home; for others, it may be a hidden source of confusion for the scattering may create a mind set of play rather than concentrated effort.

There is very little information regarding the way members of different ethnic groups feel and act under certain, preset physical arrangements. Such information seems vital to the successful variation of school and classroom design. Should all rooms have scattered chairs and desks or do members of some ethnic groups study better in more orderly situations? How close together is too close? Does physical closeness interfere with serious learning?

Sommer has given special attention to school and classroom design without, however, considering the influence of diverse ethnic backgrounds for the successful functioning of physical arrangements. He tends to assign meanings to scholastic design that come out of his own background without very much awareness of what he is doing:

> Movement in and out of classrooms and the school building itself is rigidly controlled. Everywhere one looks there are "lines"—generally straight lines that bend around corners before entering the auditorium, the cafeteria, or the shop. The linear pattern of parallel rows reinforces the lines. The straight rows tell the student to look ahead and ignore everyone except the teacher; the students are jammed so tightly together that psychological escape, much less physical separation, is impossible.[4]

Terms such as "jammed" and "psychological escape" communicate that the school design is universally unfavorable. We really do not know whether there are ethnic groups who might feel best in such situations. Psychological escape might be less necessary for members of one ethnic group than for members of another; jamming might be perceived as a "close togetherness" and be a desirable quality.

TIME MODES

We found that dealing with nonverbal mind sets, which are initially absorbed through experiences within an ethnic group but later are basic to the ways individuals orient themselves to the world irrespective of any intent to communicate with others, led us to examine how time was perceived by different ethnic groups. It is more than just a question of whether one comes late or how important it is to be on time. There seem to be important variations in the attitudes held about time and its uses by different ethnic groups; some measure accomplishments by the length of time employed, and others are seemingly unaware of time as a measurable quantity.

A personal experience might help to clarify how time can be perceived differently. While in Mexico City for a brief visit, I decided to take a trip to Cuernavaca, about thirty miles from my hotel. A friend and I hired a car and chauffeur for the brief journey, but because of a blowout, we had to return by bus. We found the bus depot but no sign giving the schedule to Mexico City. We stopped a passerby and asked in our best Spanish when the bus for Mexico City would be leaving. We were told in English, "Soon." We persisted in our effort to find out how soon was soon, but all we received was a smile and a shrug of slight confusion. We gave up and simply waited, knowing that we had no other choice. "Soon" turned out to be three hours.

We might have "made good use" of the time had we known. In light of some other experiences, I have begun to realize that making good use of time is a way I was brought up to perceive time and that its use or nonuse (at least on an hourly or daily basis) may not even occur to many Mexicans. In such a context, "soon" has only an approximate function of indicating it will not be tomorrow or next week rather than a specific function of saying you have little time in which to do anything else.

Perceptions of time have long played an important role in the schools. All kinds of study from English to gym to chemistry have normally been divided into equal periods of time during the day. The importance and/or depth of a study is in large part measured by the total number of periods dedicated to a subject. In many cases, attendance in a high school will, taken alone, assure a high school diploma. Frequently both classroom quizzes and standardized tests impose strict time limits, in terms of minutes and hours, thus adding to the learning of a subject the requirement that whatever is learned be demonstrated at a maximum rate of speed.

Whether these perceptions of time, all traditional elements of scholastic ethnicity, are beneficial or detrimental to learning in terms of the basic nature of humankind have been and continue to be the object of long debates. The perspective my students and I chose to take was one of observing similarities and differences in the uses and perceptions of time within the schools leading, possibly, to ethnic mismatches of which teachers are often unaware and which might interfere with the learning process. We wanted to know, for example, what effect the imposition or removal of time constraints would have on the quality of scholastic performance for different ethnic groups. We did not assume that imposing time constraints for learning is necessarily a negative quality for all ethnic groups. Indeed, it seemed more reasonable that members of some ethnic groups might find the imposition of time limits compatible with the mind sets for learning established during their ethnic stages of development. Whether such mind sets are or are not desirable seemed secondary to finding out what the mind sets actually are for one or another group and to determining areas of ethnic incompatibilities that need to be honestly confronted in a pluralistic public school environment.

OUTLINING ORIENTATION MODES

The outline of orientation modes is still at an initial stage of development. As far as I have been able to discern, there are sets of body and spatial arrangements that do follow group-derived patterns but do not include intentional communication. When body and spatial arrangements affect such activities as relaxation and studying, they become important considerations for

the public schools. Questions regarding the spatial arrangements most conducive to studying are especially important to
teachers. To distinguish the body and spatial arrangements of
orientation modes from those of nonverbal communication,
distinctive labels for the former have been devised: body orientations and spatial orientations.

The ways one pays attention and perceptions of time have
also been viewed as important subcategories of orientation
modes. Both their quantitative characters and qualitative differences have been considered. Thus, added to the length of
time one is capable of paying attention is the consideration of
how one pays attention, e.g., with unswerving, concentrated
linearity, with diversions of a given frequency, and so on.
Besides the perception of length of time is the attitude toward
using time, e.g., making good use of a few hours, imposing time
constraints as incentive, and the like. These subcategories have
been labelled attention modes and temporal modes.

I am by no means certain that these four subcategories are all
that should be included under the aspect of orientation modes.
We considered, for instance, the different reactions people have
toward colors and color combinations. Are such reactions only
of an individual, psychological nature, or can the influence of
one's ethnic background be discerned? We frankly did not know
and concluded their relevance to public schooling was not sufficient for inclusion as a major subcategory.

We also struggled with the process of "imprinting," which
occurs among animals when, at birth, they attach themselves to
the first moving object observed, treating it as though it were
their mother. The biological instance of "imprinting" has some
definitional affinity to the ethnically perceived category of orientation modes. However, orientation modes involve a much
more complex development based upon learnings within and
about the environment during a period of time estimated to
range from ten to twelve years. Nevertheless, we could not ignore that some form of imprinting might be present during the
ethnic development of orientation modes.[5] The dark faces and

contrasting white teeth of black parents peering into their child's crib might become meaningful as a sign of well-being, which is likely to be carried by the child into adulthood. Similarly, the brown, moon-shaped, smiling faces of Mexican-American parents may indicate well-being to the Chicano child—a well-being that no Anglo teacher could hope to duplicate. It was precisely because we felt that the aspects of imprinting that were dependent on biological traits held little promise for instructional improvement that we decided not even to attempt its inclusion. We assumed that if imprinting did occur in the early crib stages because of body or facial movements, that this would be reflected in the subcategory of body movements.

The outline of orientation modes, as far as it has been developed, is based on the premise that comparisons will be made between the orientation modes of the student, of scholastic ethnicity, and of the teacher. It is, of course, possible that certain orientation modes have no counterpart in, say, scholastic ethnicity. In such instances, mapping will have to stop after the description of a trait, and dealing instructionally with the trait will mean developing methodologies that are either compatible with or take advantage of the trait in question.

FOOTNOTES

[1]Mark L. Knapp, *Nonverbal Communication in Human Interaction* (New York: Holt, Rinehart and Winston, 1972).

[2]Ibid., pp. 98-99.

[3]Robert Sommer, *Personal Space: The Behavioral Basic of Design* (Englewood Cliffs: Prentice-Hall, 1969) p. 46.

[4]Ibid., p. 99.

[5]Professor Leonard Olguin, in a presentation at The University of Michigan-Flint, emphasized the importance of imprinting for the development of Mexican-American youth, 1973.

ORIENTATION MODES

A. Body Orientations
    1. Relaxation
    2. Study
    3. Other

B. Spatial Architectural Orientations
    1. Relaxation
    2. Study
    3. Other

C. Attention Modes
    1. Span Capability
       a. Classroom situation
       b. Independent study situation
    2. Variations in quality of span
       a. Classroom situation
       b. Independent study situation
    3. Other

D. Time Modes
    1. Perceptions of uses and nature
    2. Diversity in perceptions of length
    3. Other

Using the above outline, comparative studies may be undertaken per the following model:

Orientation Modes Native to Student or Group of Students in a School	(Possibility of) Orientation Modes Inherent in Scholastic Ethnicity	Orientation Modes Native to Teacher or Group of Teachers in a School

CHAPTER VII

Social Value Patterns

The ethnic aspect of social value patterns is based on the sets of persistent behaviors that a group expects from its members and upon which it places certain values and upholds with certain beliefs. If a teenage boy whose family is short of money finds a job, the taking of that job probably reflects his rational assessment of his financial needs and would not normally be considered an ethnically developed social value pattern. On the other hand, if a high percentage of teenagers belonging to a particular group seeks employment while they are still students, despite such factors as having no financial need or being slow students who need more time for study, there is a good likelihood that a group-held, ethnically developed social value pattern is operating. Assuming the existence of a general American ethnicity, the view that all able-bodied men should work, regardless of whether there is a need, would belong to a social value pattern revolving around work. Other behaviors that might be observed in a group's work pattern could relate to the status attributed to a job, the proper forms of competition among fellow workers, the frequency with which new employment is sought, and the rules established for retirement.

SOCIAL VALUE PATTERNS

All ethnic groupings normally establish social practices to which members are expected to conform in specific ways. The original need for these practices and their prescribed behaviors may, in time, be significantly altered or even disappear, but they have become traditions and, as such, they are transferred ethnically to the young who learn these behaviors prior to the development of their abstract reasoning powers or the ability to judge the qualities of the traditions they are learning. Thus, social value patterns may continue to survive as powerful molders of the way adults behave, notwithstanding significant shifts in their ideas that may occur with maturity.

This is not to say that mature analysis does not effect tradition or ethnic development, but this is more apparent between generations rather than within the same generation. To take a hypothetical instance, let's say that Jean had been brought up as a bigot—bigotry is in the very texture of her ethnic background. As she matured and came to realize, in an objective fashion, the injustices her prejudices caused, she consciously rejected behaviors that arose from her ethnically absorbed bigotry. However, she probably would not be able to overcome certain gut-level reactions she might have, say, toward blacks. Although Jean supports the idea of desegregated restaurants, she would probably frequent restaurants having only a white clientele, or be shocked, quietly inside, to see a black at the next table. She would probably continue to be surprised to see a well-dressed, handsome black who talks the way a Harvard professor might, no matter how often such incidents may be repeated, and she would never feel relaxed enough when talking to a black to chat as she might to any of her many white acquaintances.

This inability to control inner reactions is probably at the heart of the interracial and interethnic hypocrisy that afflicts our present-day efforts to achieve equal opportunity: "We're not prejudiced, we just could not find a first-rate black who would fit the position as well as the white we hired," and the like. What Jean is able to do in her rational effort to overcome the bigotry taught to her ethnically is avoid behaving like a bigot in front of her children—at least, not act as much like a bigot as her parents did in front of her. This exercise of control over what an adult says and does when children are present can undermine the ethnic transferral of bigotry between generations. Indeed, it may happen that children, who will know their parents' foibles, will recognize the ethnic remnants of their bigotry and accuse them of hypocrisy.

WAYS GROUPS SUSTAIN SOCIAL VALUE PATTERNS

This intergenerational process effecting changes in social value patterns of ethnic development obviously does not happen to all members of an ethnic group at the same time nor with the same intensity. This means that even if a majority consensus about a specific set of behaviors exists in a group, there would be undercurrents of beliefs and behaviors that would differ or even run counter to those generally acknowledged. In other words, within the context of the same ethnic group, there would be *dominant patterns* engaged in by a majority and *secondary patterns* engaged in by many members but not a majority. Simply because a secondary social value pattern is observed does not mean that it will continue to strengthen until it becomes a dominant pattern; it may remain a secondary undercurrent or even disappear from the scene.

Social value patterns may be widely discussed and overtly supported by an ethnic group, in which case they can be considered *manifest patterns,* or they may be infrequently discussed and covertly supported, in which case they can be thought of as *latent patterns.* This distinction between the latent and the manifest with regard to beliefs and values was made as far back as the 1920s by Thorstein Veblen in *The Theory of the Leisure Class.* Veblen noted that although the reason usually given by people for buying expensive goods is because they are of better quality, they have other latent reasons such as that expensive goods reflect a high social status.[1] In this instance, the undercurrent of desiring higher social status may remain latent because of a direct conflict with at least two other manifest social value patterns: one, the practice of thrift and avoidance of wastefulness in the use of goods, and the other, of being simple and unassuming and not coveting worldly riches or praise.

It must be emphasized that just because beliefs and values are latent does not mean that the behaviors they induce are not part of a dominant pattern followed by a majority of members of the group. Since Veblen wrote his book, the pattern of wasteful consumption has steadily increased in dominance, even though the values and beliefs supporting wastefulness were not widely discussed and the pattern of wastefulness thus remained latent. In other words, though not talked about much, wastefulness became a dominant way of acting. In recent times, wastefulness, now called conspicuous consumption, energy guzzling, and the like, has become a manifest pattern, and the values and beliefs supporting it have been frequently discussed.

Indeed, the fact that wastefulness has become a manifest pattern may lead to its undoing as a dominant pattern. The rationale underlying the drive for increased conservation is so clear to almost all adults that they are likely to pass on to their children concepts of wastefulness very different from those learned in their own childhood. This is likely to happen even though many of these same adults are still acting according to the molds of their early upbringing, as can be evidenced in the surge of large car sales and the subsequent decline in small car sales of the late 1970s. Although public warnings continue regarding the pending oil shortage, mature adults cannot easily overcome their ethnically developed social value pattern of conspicuous consumption, which is a clear form of wastefulness. Part of the difficulty may be the long period of latency of this present dominant pattern. Latency conceals or, at least obscures, the values and beliefs supporting a behavioral pattern. What is absorbed as a child is never formulated into clearly stated reasons and, therefore, what needs to be unlearned is obscure.

There is still another kind of perspective from which a group's participation in its social value patterns may be viewed. All groups hold beliefs and values about the behavior expected from the group as a whole; they also hold beliefs and values about expected patterns that apply primarily to the behavior of individual members of the group. Group oriented expectations and individually oriented expectations may not be fully consistent with each other. For instance, a given ethnic group may have a dominant, manifest belief that all its members should follow the established laws; this same group may also have another dominant, manifest belief that a man should defend his marital honor even to the extent of beating his adulterous wife or murdering his wife's lover, both of which violate laws supported by the group. Justice may take such personal circumstances into account, even to the point of not inflicting punishment on the man, but the group may still not excuse him for having violated another deeply felt, albeit contradictory, social value pattern. A logical recognition, which adults would probably have, of the conflict existing between group and individual expectations might mitigate the group's reactions but probably not overcome them.

In Italy's recent history is an example of the kind of tension that can develop between group and individually oriented patterns. American newspapers have referred widely to Italy's new law permitting divorce. It has been estimated that approximately 5,000,000 couples were affected when the law passed. This meant that 10,000,000 people in a population of about 70,000,000 were living together out of wedlock. If only married couples are taken into account, somewhere in the neighborhood of one-fourth of those living together were *not* abiding by the dominant, manifest marital social value pattern, which holds that the sanctity of marriage goes beyond individual happiness and is a duty to the group as a whole and to the God it worships. The social value patterns effectively disregarded by 10,000,000 people were those related to the age-old prohibition against divorce. The pattern of living together out of wedlock was a secondary one, which was not latent, although somewhat less manifest than the one prohibiting divorce.

The fact that Italians as a whole seemed to have widely accepted out-of-wedlock unions indicates that another social value pattern of a conflicting nature is operating. This pattern is likely to be at the individual level and may be a dominant one.

Italians, both in their history and their literature, seem to perceive of individual daily living as a series of survival tactics from which a little happiness may be grasped before a major disaster happens. Individuals must squeeze what happiness they can from life out of a multitude of obligations thrust upon them. Only God can judge how right they are—priests really cannot do this.

Another individually oriented, though definitely dominant, pattern that seems to be present is the perception of a true man as a romantic lover. A normal man, even if married, is expected to remain a Romeo, who, in the actual experience of going after other women, may fall in love with one to the point of leaving his socially accepted marital situation and grasping what happiness life may still hold for him. Prizing romantic passion over the deadliness of daily life is a social value pattern understood and often upheld by large numbers of Italians. It creates a counter tension to the dominant, manifest, and publicly oriented pattern prohibiting divorce, which is based on a set of religious moral values and beliefs.

PRIZING AND MORAL VALUING

The inconsistencies reflected in such social value patterns as divorce arise only in part from the different ways a group participates in these patterns. In large part, the inconsistencies must be laid to the very nature of values—to the different kinds of goals toward which an act of valuing may be directed. Valuing includes prizings as well as moral valuing. Prizings may run the gamut from mere preferences ("I like ice cream.") to estimates of worth in concrete as well as abstract terms ("What is it worth to me?") to most deeply felt cherishings ("I shall always cherish this memory."). Like prizings, moral values may range from minor requirements ("I agreed to be there at 10:00 p.m.") to important obligations ("My contract imposes many legal obligations upon me.") to basic moral ideals ("I shall do the Lord's bidding because what He wants is good.").

Prizings and moral valuing may be present simultaneously and even with equal weight for opposing patterns of behavior. For example, it is a moral ideal not to steal; it is also a prizing to have wealth and material goods. The latter may be of so much concrete worth that the moral value of not stealing may be ignored. To reinforce the moral ideal, a law prohibiting stealing may be passed.

Of course, prizings and moral valuing are often consistent with each other. For example, an ethnic group may both prize and believe in the moral ideal of working to the best of one's ability. Doing kindnesses for others may have religious moral value, but it is also cherished as a sign of sincere friendship. Whether a simultaneous presence of moral value and prizing would make a social value pattern more pervasive or powerful has not yet been explored in the present study, but the author certainly suspects that that is the case.

ESTIMATING DESIRABILITY, IMPORTANCE, AND POSSIBILITY

It must be recognized that a group is always *evaluating* its social value patterns. Depending on what is believed, a set of behaviors may be seen as desirable or undesirable, as important to achieve or as unimportant, as possible to accomplish or as impossible. Each of these three ways of evaluating forms a continuum covering a gamut from very desirable to very undesirable, from very important to very unimportant, from fully possible to absolutely impossible. Furthermore, each of the three represents a type of evaluation; thus, the very desirable to very undesirable continuum could also be perceived as a very-acceptable to not-at-all-acceptable continuum, and the very-important to not-very-important continuum might be expressed in terms of a very-necessary to not-at-all-necessary continuum depending upon the context within which a set of behaviors occurs.

An example may help clarify these evaluative distinctions.

Wastefulness as an individually oriented pattern of conspicuous consumption may be somewhat desirable as a way of showing economic status, not too important to accomplish but very easy or possible to achieve. Conservation as a group oriented pattern may be very desirable and very important but not easily accomplished because of its dependence on the compliance of individual members of the group. Wastefulness has been a dominant but latent pattern expressed mostly as a preference, while conservation has been a secondary but manifest pattern perceived as an obligation to the future. The conflicting and dovetailing aspects of conservation and wastefulness have made rational analyses of the values and beliefs underlying these patterns extremely difficult. What is more, because conspicuous consumption has been an individually oriented pattern while conservation has been a group oriented pattern, changes in values held about one have not necessarily changed the evaluation or nature of values held about the other. In other words, because the pattern refers to the group rather than individuals, or vice versa, and because it is absorbed ethnically, it seems possible to ignore logical connections between patterns and their beliefs and values. We all seem to be capable of incorporating inconsistent and even conflicting social value patterns and to behave in contradictory ways without being fully aware of what we are doing.

USES OF SOCIAL VALUE PATTERN DESCRIPTORS

If the discussion of social value patterns has been overly concerned with generalized qualities that can describe patterns regardless of their content, it is because I am painfully aware of the complexity of trying to describe objectively sets of persistent behaviors and the beliefs and values on which they are based. Any search for beliefs and values is liable to the biases of the observer, and this is especially true when the area studied covers such a potentially vast range of human behavior. Furthermore, whatever is observed is filtered through the unique circumstances and personalities of those being observed, so that even if perfect objectivity were achieved by the observers, the individual subjectivity of those being observed would be an integral part of any observation.

To encompass this inherent subjectivity as well as the mind-boggling complexity of social value patterns, I have sought categorical descriptors from which essential questions about discerned patterns of social behavior could be derived. To some degree, these questions are implicit in the characteristics stipulated for behaviors to be recognized as a social value pattern. For instance, behaviors acquired during the ethnic stages of development lead to the question of *when* a set of behaviors might be learned by the members of a group; behaviors forming a discernible pattern repeated with some frequency lead to the questions of *how frequent* a pattern is and how fixed the sequence of behaviors are. Our continuing development of descriptors of social value patterns is an effort to achieve more complete guidelines regarding what questions need to be asked to characterize a social value pattern.

In general, the development of descriptors or subcategories has been directed toward the exploration of *differences* in the ways groups engage in and evaluate their patterns as well as toward possible differences in the nature of the values present. Most ethnic groups embrace nationally accepted norms and formats for marriage, divorce, and the like, which tend to hide some of the real differences in what is believed and valued. Within the context of schooling, institutional authority in the form of classroom discipline may be widely accepted by diverse ethnic groups, even though the actual perceptions of what are acceptable forms of discipline and what are important areas for discipline may vary a great deal from one group to another. Teachers tend not to be aware of such differences. They may treat such activities as gum chewing very differently depending on their age (period when they were brought up), their ethnic group membership, the geographic location where they grew up, and the like. Because of such differences among teachers as well as among students, the application of school discipline may be very uneven.

Teaching birth control is an instance within the school where unintended problems may arise because differences in social value patterns are overlooked. Can the public schools deal with such emotionally charged questions as birth control in an objective fashion for all students without deeply offending or confusing the members of some ethnic groups? What can teachers do in their instructional methodology to ease the conflicts that might arise in children of different ethnic backgrounds? Obviously, before such questions can be faced, increased understanding of the differences that exist in social value patterns relating to birth control would need to be achieved.

Some initial efforts to organize objective descriptions of differences have been undertaken, but to date they are only exploratory, and the results have never been incorporated into an ethnic profile. The system is based on the three sets of descriptors: *1)* types of participation (dominant/secondary, manifest/latent, group oriented/individually oriented); *2)* evaluation of social value patterns (desirable/undesirable, important/unimportant, possible/impossible); and *3)* nature of valuing (prizing/moralizing).

To illustrate, a hypothetical case was presented to members of an ethnic group: a fourteen-year-old boy is in danger of failing a course while all of his friends are doing well; he cheats on the next test and receives a much better grade. Respondents were asked a set of questions about cheating on the exam reflective of the three sets of descriptors. The answers were estimated along each of the continuums, which were turned into scales:

1. Under the circumstances, how acceptable or unacceptable is the act of cheating?

Acceptable				Unacceptable
1	2	3	4	5

2. Given the average circumstances of youngsters you know, how important is it for this boy's family that he do well on the exam?

Important				Unimportant
1	2	3	4	5

3. Given what you know about schools and about boys in your own circle of friends and relatives, how easily or possible would it be for the boy to cheat on the test?

Possible				Impossible
1	2	3	4	5

The questions were worded to elicit the values and beliefs that a respondent might personally hold regarding a given behavior (such as cheating).

If a number of respondents have been identified as belonging to a given ethnic group, the median of the responses may be noted along the 1-5 continuum. If more than one question can be devised about one of the continuums, then the average point between the median points from responses to each question may be placed along that one continuum. For example, in addition to the above question 3, the following could be asked: "Given what you know about schools and about boys in your own circle of friends and relatives, how probable is it that the boy would cheat on the test?" The median point obtained from this question would be averaged with the median point obtained from the first question so that there would still be only one point in the continuum.

Since each of the above continuums is a way of evaluating a social value pattern, an ethnic group's *evaluative perspective* of a given social value pattern may be depicted by a line connecting the median response points (or average of median response points) of the continuums. (This assumes that each of the three evaluators—desirable, important, and possible—are of equal significance, which really may not be the case.)

Cheating on Test:
Linear Representation of Median
Evaluating Response

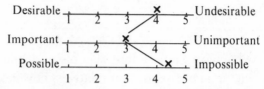

This "picture" of an ethnic group's evaluative perspective may be compared to the responses that another ethnic group might make to the same case and the same questions. In this way, a visual representation of differences may be established, which would allow a second set of discrete questions to be investigated, such as whether an observable difference in the linear representations of two ethnic groups correlates to differences in actual behaviors related to cheating on tests.

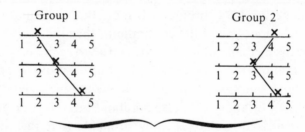

Do the differences in these linear "pictures" represent some kind of predictable difference in cheating behaviors?

This graphing of median points was extended to include the sets of descriptors indicating how a group perceives its participation in a social value pattern as well as the nature of the valuing involved. For instance, a question referring to the dominant/secondary continuum might be: "Based on your own experience with boys in your family or in the families of friends and neighbors, how many youngsters do you think would cheat under the circumstances described?" Most? A majority? Fifty-fifty? Less than a majority? Few? The median of the responses received could then be placed on a dominant/ secondary continuum. Following the procedures outlined for the evaluative perspective, a *participation or sustaining perspective* might be developed as in the following example:

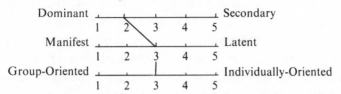

This effort to visualize differences in social value patterns endeavors to achieve intersubjectivity so that teachers may discuss, in an objective fashion, potential areas of incompatibility among the social value patterns held by different ethnic groups. The approach is still evolving, and several methods for bringing the sets of descriptors together in a single graphic representation are being explored as is the possibility of finding some kind of numerical representation for each. Further discussion regarding these explorations can be found in Appendix B.

Even without attempting to achieve visual or numerical representations of social value patterns, the three sets of descriptors provide a rational source of questions that may be used either in interviews with members of a group or as guides for observation in the classroom. For example, Peter wears a hat to class every day. A few other youngsters of the same ethnic group, though not a majority, also wear their hats in class. The practice seems to have individually oriented meaning, but the students have difficulty explaining the underlying value. Nevertheless, they cherish wearing their hats and consider this a reasonably acceptable activity that is also important for their image among their peers as well as perfectly possible. "Hat-wearing" could thus be assigned the following descriptors:

    -secondary; latent; individually-oriented
    -prizing value (cherishing)
    -acceptable; important; possible

The teacher, on the other hand, is a woman who grew up believing men should remove their hats indoors and that this is a sign of respect. The act of removing a hat for purposes of showing respect may also be associated with the Christian practice of men removing their hats in church. Thus, the teacher may perceive of wearing a hat in class as undesirable because it is rude and also unacceptable because it may interfere with other students being able to see in the room. Her view of the behavior may classify it as an unimportant preference that students could modify with little cost to themselves. "Hat-wearing" from the teacher's perspective could be assigned the following descriptors:

-secondary; latent; individually-oriented
-prizing value (preference)
- { unacceptable
  { undesirable: unimportant; possible

The likelihood for a clash arising from the two diverse social value patterns related to dress is clear, but is it avoidable? Might not a teacher who is aware of these differences arrange for students who wish to wear their hats to class to sit at the back or sides of a room? If the hats must be removed, could this not be requested with the kindness suitable to asking someone to give up something they cherish? Could it not be explained that many groups in the United States would interpret wearing a hat in the classroom as disrespectful? I suspect most teachers would respond affirmatively to the latter questions, if they were sufficiently aware of how their own social value pattern regarding hats worn indoors differs from that of the student.

ORGANIZING SOCIAL VALUE PATTERNS

Although the descriptors and their related questions offer a way of dealing with social value patterns with increased objectivity and with a set of common guidelines that can be used in a similar fashion by all researchers, the number of possible social value patterns was still beyond the ability of my students to cope with practically. They did collect only behavioral patterns likely to have developed during the ethnic stages of childhood; they did eliminate behavioral patterns that were not observed frequently. Still, the gamut of behaviors that might be observed, collected, and generalized about was too broad.

It was decided to limit observations to those social value patterns most likely to influence behavior in the classroom or on the school grounds. Some of these varied, depending on whether an elementary or secondary school were involved, while others remained essentially the same regardless of grade level.

Among those patterns the average teacher might observe are: *friendship patterns,* (including small group leadership, gang relationships, boy-girl relationships, and trust); *educational patterns* (attitudes toward and accomplishments in scholastic achievement, expectations from formal schooling, and reactions to institutional setting); *family patterns* (especially father-mother responsibility toward children in school, obligations of school-age youngsters to meet family needs, and status of younger and older male and female siblings in family); *employment patterns* (including frequent geographic relocation, type and frequency of part-time employment among school-aged youngsters, and employment aspirations of students); and *delinquency patterns* (including types of discipline problems most frequent in school, differentiations among school-aged youngsters regarding serious and not-so-serious crime, and extra-legal ethical standards). Other important areas of social value patterns such as dress might present themselves in the course of classroom observations, and the preceding list would, of course, be extended.

Because each of the five aspects of ethnicity is qualitatively different from the other aspects, the outline devised for each has a distinctive form and set of inquiries. Verbal communication and nonverbal communication, which both involve messages shared between people, are the most similar. Even so, the outlines reflect the different stages of study reached for the two aspects so that "ethnic criteria for judging verbal communication . . ." is explicitly included in verbal communication while it is implicit in nonverbal communication.

Retrieval and inquiry functions are simultaneously served by all the subheadings of the outlines for these two aspects, as well as for orientation modes and intellectual modes (to be discussed in the next chapter). Such is *not* the case for social value patterns; because of the necessity for merging beliefs and values with empirically observable activities, the proposed outline uses the subcategories or descriptors somewhat differently. The retrieval function is served primarily by the areas of study that are developed as the need arises. For example, it has been suggested that delinquency patterns, family patterns, and employment patterns might be among the most useful areas of study for teachers. These areas are further distinguished by indicating patterns of a student's heritage, of scholastic ethnicity, and of the teacher's heritage. These retrieval categories might guide observation, but for the most part they are not expected to be effective since observers themselves would create the categories when a need is felt. The main body of the social value patterns' outline functions as a set of inquiries about the types of tensions that arise within and between patterns and that may sometimes produce contradictory or unclear ethnic behaviors within a group and conflict between groups. The outline assumes a complexity of intra-and inter-group tensions that can be clarified by the description of single patterns and subsequent comparisons.

Comparisons should be both *vertical* and *horizontal* in nature. That is, several social value patterns held by students could be developed to gain insights into the ethnic conflicts that a youngster may be involved in quite independently of school. This is a vertical study. Horizontal comparisons would compare the vertical patterns of the student, the teacher, and scholastic ethnicity in one particular area to ascertain possible conflicts.

FOOTNOTE

[1]Thorstein Veblen, *The Theory of the Leisure Class* (New York: Vanguard Press, 1928) p. 25.

SOCIAL VALUE PATTERNS

A. Ways of Participating in Patterns
   1. Group-oriented/individually-
      oriented continuum
   2. Dominant/secondary continuum
   3. Manifest/latent continuum

B. Ways of Evaluating Patterns
   1. Desirable/undesirable
      continuum
   2. Important/unimportant
      continuum
   3. Possible/impossible continuum

C. Nature of Valuing
   1. Prizing
      a. Preference
      b. Worth
      c. Cherishing
   2. Moral Valuing
      a. Minor requirement
      b. Obligation
      c. Moral ideal

Using the above outline, specific areas of concern, such as delinquency patterns or friendship patterns, may be compared horizontally per the following model:

DELINQUENCY PATTERNS:

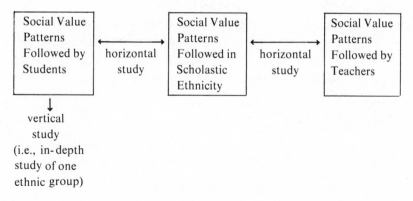

CHAPTER VIII

Intellectual Modes

Intellectual modes are the most emotionally charged aspect of ethnicity that my students and I dealt with. We had to repeatedly extricate ourselves from the debates of geneticists, psychologists, and educators concerning whether human intelligence is predetermined by inherited factors[1] or is dependent primarily upon environmental factors for the depth and breadth of its development.

The aspect of intellectual modes is not intended, in any way, to deal with human innate intelligence, whatever it may be, if it exists at all. Berelson and Steiner, among many scholars, have noted the present inability to deal with native intelligence minus social experience: "Raw native capacity, unaffected by learning, is as impossible to measure as it is to observe (since there are no people without experience)."[2] Thus, this category is intended to deal with observable intellectual performances.

The unique qualities of a group's ethnicity lie in the shared social experiences of its members. As educational experiments in intellectual performance have multiplied, it has become increasingly apparent that children's perceptions, ability to use cues, reasoning ability, and the like are all influenced by their experiences. Among the conclusions listed in Berelson's and Steiner's inventory of scientific studies concerning intellectual performance are:

People more readily discriminate between things they have different names for. . . .[3]

Connotations are remarkably similar among similar people.[4]

Problems are difficult to solve when they require the use of the familiar in an unfamiliar way.[5]

Things important to remember are remembered better than things that do not make any difference ("importance" defined subjectively).[6]

.. general social attitudes (e.g., stereotypes) influence memory. . . .[7]

Each conclusion, either directly or indirectly, links intellectual performance to past experience. It is as members of an ethnic group that individuals first internalize what is important, establish the set of things for which there are names, make some objects and acts usual while others remain unusual, and achieve social attitudes. The shared experiences of an ethnic group must be highly influential for individual intellectual performance.

The basic assumption of the aspect of intellectual modes is that regardless of genetic differences, the way children externalize their thoughts can be linked to their ethnic group. In other words, intellect will be expressed through behaviors that are acquired during the ethnic stages of development. To some extent these behaviors reflect social value patterns concerning the most desirable, important, and possible ways of using intelligence. However, they are absorbed so early and used so completely without awareness in pre-school children that they become a structural part of the way they externalize their thoughts about things—how they approach a problem, what they give their full attention, the details they are most likely to recall, or the types of questions they are likely to use while learning. In this sense, this category is also akin to orientation modes and the ways children learn to pay attention or study effectively. The aspect of intellectual modes is distinguished primarily by limiting its observations specifically to the performances of intellectual abilities, such as engaging in quantitative analyses or memorizing a certain type of data or resolving a problem of spatial organization, and the kinds of contexts in which these skills are performed poorly, not at all, or quite well.

INFLUENCE OF ETHNICITY ON THE EXERCISE
OF INTELLECTUAL ABILITIES

The influence of ethnicity on intellectual modes may be seen operating on at least three levels: *1)* how learning is approached or undertaken: *2)* assigning importance or emphasis to some intellectual abilities and overlooking or giving little emphasis to other intellectual abilities: and *3)* establishing the kinds of contexts and activities in which the exercise of certain intellectual abilities are favored or expected.

In practical classroom terms, the first of the three levels, how learning is approached, might be observed when a bright young Jewish student, brought up in the New York City area, asks numerous questions of a teacher who is trying to present some new, relatively complex idea to a class. Within the context of scholastic ethnicity, the teacher would probably expect quiet attention until the presentation is completed, after which questions would be in order. On the other hand, a young Jewish child growing up in New York City engages in a very different learning mode. At home, he or she is continually invited to ask questions about what is being taught while it is being taught. The "teacher" repeatedly asks: "Do you know what I mean?" "What do you think of that?" "Are you sure you understand what I have said up to this point?" Youngsters who are brought up expecting to question and discuss while new learning is going on are likely to upset not only non-Jewish public school teachers but other students in the class who have different ethnic heritages. Many of their classmates ethnically need uninterrupted presentations, especially when they involve complex ideas. Were a teacher to become aware of an intellectual learning mode such as I have described, some remedy might be sought that would respect the multi-ethnic composition of the class. The teacher might, for example, ask Jewish youngsters to write down their questions as they think of them so that they may be discussed later. Indeed, students might exchange their questions with each other and decide together which ones still need to be answered at the end of the presentation.

Other types of approaches to learning deal with the kinds of questions that are asked, the way problems are treated, and the way information is organized and perceived. For example, is an article written in a factual style accepted as factual without any doubt or question? Are problems considered puzzles to be solved or unpleasant interludes?

Assigning importance to certain intellectual abilities might mean in practice that an ethnic group gives importance to developing fluency in verbal expression while underplaying numerical skills. Oral fluency might be emphasized over written expression. The group might further emphasize oral skills of a comic or ironic variety as opposed to poetic expressions of a romantic variety. Even those who seem to have an individual propensity for poetic romanticism, will probably reflect, in the performance of their verbal skills, the emphasis placed on irony by their group.

Even when a group obviously emphasizes abilities related to oral fluency, there are likely to be contexts that favor or impede the exercise of such abilities. Consider controversial political discussions, which are often part of a classroom activity. From the perspective of social value patterns, they may be something to avoid in public and may actually impede the exercise of skills related to oral fluency in the youngsters of some ethnic groups. On the other hand, role playing without a pre-established script may be an excellent vehicle for increasing the oral fluency of students from some groups. In sum, intellectual modes describe how learning is approached, which intellectual abilities are emphasized, and the quality(s) of the ability emphasized and the acts and contexts within which it is either favored or inhibited.

INTELLECTUAL ASPECTS OF
SCHOLASTIC ETHNICITY

Scholastic ethnicity has its own set of intellectual modes, separate and sometimes very distinct from the modes of a student's ethnic heritage. The intellectual modes of scholastic ethnicity were established long ago. Standardized tests and national norms are the embodiment of these modes. The intellectual abilities emphasized by the I.Q. tests are consistent with the intellectual operations necessary to succeed in school subjects, especially those leading to college. The intellectual experiences of students in their pre-school stage of ethnic development have been disregarded for so long that not even the characteristics of middle-class, white Anglo youngsters are picked up intentionally by the schools in their quest to develop the intellect. The intellectual modes of one's ethnic heritage may be quite similar to those fostered in traditional school subjects; they may also be quite different. The schools simply have not examined sufficiently the influence of ethnicity on intellectual performance or the relationship of the patterns developed in the pre-school ethnic stage to those patterns supported by the traditional subjects. Adopting different patterns of intellectual performance has not been seriously entertained by the schools.

Because my students and I took the present public school environment as the setting for our action research, we mapped our investigations of intellectual performance around the kinds of performance most often emphasized by public schools when developing achievement and aptitude profiles for their students. These are:

> Verbal fluency
> Numerical ability
> Spatial reasoning
> Mechanical reasoning
> Abstract reasoning

Each of these is a conglomeration of mental abilities organized according to similarities in observable intellectual performance. In verbal fluency the capacity of individuals to manipulate vocabulary and syntax cogently and/or creatively is the fulcrum of a number of skills; in numerical ability the capacity to work in diverse ways with quantities links a variety of skills together; in spatial reasoning skills related to the development and manipulation of forms and their spatial relationships are brought together; in mechanical reasoning the skills used in applying physical principles to concrete problem situations (as occurs with machinery or building construction) are studied; and in abstract reasoning the skills involved in manipulating symbols, concepts, and ideas are examined along with the skills used in deriving principles from a series of experiences.

Along with the five complex skills listed above, we added another classification of intellectual abilities—memory. We felt that retention of information was not only vital to all the other classifications, it was also greatly influenced by past experiences, which in young school children are their ethnic development. We all seem to remember best those things we believe are important and with which we are familiar. Knowing the contexts and the acts within which a youngster achieves her or his best level of retention could be of significance to daily instructional planning for a teacher could plan into a lesson performances reflective of children's backgrounds.

The set of intellectual skills fostered in the schools was taken as the departure point for viewing the various influences of ethnicity on intellectual development. The question of how learning is approached was made more specific, e.g., how is learning in verbal fluency, numerical ability, and the other abilities approached? The question of ethnic emphasis may be, which of the six scholastic abilities is most emphasized by the ethnic group? A reasonable follow-up question would be, what intellectual abilities are emphasized by the group but not by the schools?

Of all the aspects of ethnicity, intellectual modes is the most difficult to come to grips with. Besides the emotional tension generated by the proposition that intellectual ability is inherited and not liable to environmental enrichment, there is real uncertainty about what the important intellectual abilities are that ought to be encouraged by the schools. The skills emphasized by I.Q. tests might well be replaced by another set of intellectual skills as even Arthur R. Jensen, a foremost proponent of the genetic thesis, admits.[8] The public school's emphasis on certain kinds of intellectual operations is a choice, not a biological necessity. It has long been noted, for instance, that a creative artist performs only slightly better than average on most I.Q. tests, indicating that the tests are not measuring intellectual skills that lead to successful creative performance. Such skills as being able to ask key questions also seem to be reflected poorly in I.Q. tests. Conscious revisions of the intellectual modes typifying scholastic ethnicity may be in order. In any event, we took the existing situation as our departure point.

Teachers, under present circumstances, are the only bridge between the intellectual modes fostered by the schools and those brought to schools by youngsters of a pluralistic society. A teacher's own background may frequently interfere with his or her capacity to help students to overcome whatever gap may exist between the intellectual modes of their heritage and the modes of scholastic ethnicity. In part, teachers are probably unaware of their own modes or those implied by the school's curriculum and subsequent forms of evaluation. In part they may be questioning the very skills being emphasized by the school and may believe creative skills should be fostered rather than those typically encouraged. A systematic effort to understand the intellectual modes favored by scholastic ethnicity, by the ethnicity of the student's heritage, and by the ethnicity of the teacher's own heritage would assist teachers to develop classroom methodologies that would help students overcome what might otherwise be self-defeating conflicts between several ethnically different intellectual modes. To develop bridges does not mean that eventually students' intellectual modes would be transformed or eliminated, but rather that control over a broader range of intellectual patterns would be achieved.

The following outline is intended to help in a systematic comparison of the intellectual modes held by students, teachers, and scholastic ethnicity. As in the other aspects, an effort has been made to achieve a description of the patterns involved when learning occurs in one or another ability for each of the three ethnicities. This may be considered the in-depth or vertical approach to studying intellectual modes. Subsequently, if possible, comparisons between the modes of different ethnicities would be undertaken in what may be called a horizontal analysis. The purpose of the horizontal analysis would be to ascertain possible sources of conflict students might encounter as well as real strengths of an ethnic group's intellectual modes so that these may be included in daily lesson planning.

FOOTNOTES

[1] Fervent support for genetically fixed intelligence has been given in such articles as "How Much Can We Boost I.Q. and Scholastic Achievement?" by Arthur R. Jensen, *Harvard Educational Review,* Vol. 39, No. 1 Winter 1969, pp. 1-123; and "I.Q." by Richard J. Herrnstein, *The Atlantic,* Vol. 228, No. 3, September 1971, pp. 43-64.

[2] Bernard Berelson and Gary A. Steiner, *Human Behavior: An Inventory of Scientific Findings* (New York: Harcourt, Brace and World, 1964) p. 209.

[3] Ibid., p. 190.

[4] Ibid., p. 200.

[5] Ibid., p. 203

[6] Ibid., p. 181

[7] Ibid., p. 185.

[8] Jenson, *op. cit.,* p. 19.

INTELLECTUAL MODES

A. Ethnic Influence on Approach to Learning

    1. Behavior during new learning
    2. Questioning styles
    3. Ways of dealing with different kinds of problems
    4. Ways of organizing data
    5. Other

B. Ethnic Emphasis Favoring Development of Intellectual Abilities

    1. Preferences in abilities
    2. Qualities emphasized in exercise of intellectual abilities (e.g., individual oral performance emphasized in verbal fluency)
    3. Other

C. Typical Contexts and Activities

    1. Activities likely to favor/impede development of given intellectual ability
    2. Settings likely to favor/impede development of given intellectual ability

Using the above outline, comparative studies may be undertaken per the following model:

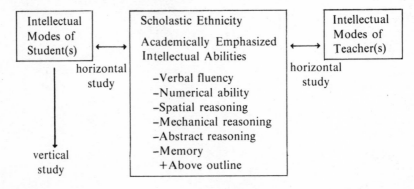

CHAPTER IX

Action Researching

The ethnic profile, as we call the five aspects of ethnicity, offered us a way of mapping or arranging our observations so that generalizations about the ethnicity of a group could be developed. As the number of inputs into a profile increased, it was assumed that the reliability of the generalizations made would also increase, though not necessarily in direct proportion. It was further assumed that all generalizations would remain tentative and subject to continual revision. In other words, it was acknowledged from the beginning that scientifically demonstrable data about ethnic behavior was not a likely outcome. We were working toward achieving the most reasonable hypotheses possible about a group's patterns of behavior rather than toward establishing a set of conclusions.

There were at least three important reasons for taking this posture of "ongoing tentativeness:"

1. *Data Subjectivity.* The direct observations of teachers, which are a major source of data for the ethnic profile, necessarily reflect the subjective involvement of teachers with what they are observing, even if precautions are taken to eliminate the most blatant aspects of their subjectivity. Subjectivity can be mitigated by increasing the number of observers of diverse ethnic backgrounds who observe the same activities or by making use of different kinds of data sources referring to similar activities, or by pre-determining the procedures to be followed during observations. However, since there is at present no way of measuring the

degrees of subjectivity brought to observations by observers of different ethnic backgrounds or from different
kinds of data sources, there is no way of determining the
correct mix of observations necessary or the "right" format to ensure objectivity. In other words, while precautions are taken, they are not sufficient.

2. *Data Instability.* It has to be assumed that the ethnic behaviors observed will undergo significant changes (even if external environmental conditions were to remain unchanged) as a result of the exercise of human will. While
physical scientists must contend with the risk of change,
they have been able to exclude as a change agent the will of
the objects they study. In the study of human behavior, the
operations of individual and group will are constantly
present and cannot be excluded. Significant shifts in a
group's ethnic patterns are obviously linked to the exercise
of human will, which is poorly understood and not presently predictable.

3. *Methodological Uncertainty.* A conclusive study of even
one aspect of ethnicity for a single ethnic group will not be
possible since the definition of ethnicity and each of the
aspects is avowedly tentative and subject to continual modification. Besides, conclusiveness would be beyond the possibilities of teachers. While they are teaching, they are also
observing. This dual role not only leads to subjectivity in
observing, but limits significantly the number and kinds of
observations that can be made. Sampling techniques must
also be eliminated in the public school situation. The
amount of time available, the number of observers participating, the students observed, the uncertainty of definitions, and the quality of skills in using the ethnic profile by
the various observers would all be indeterminant variants
potentially undermining the reliability of the outcomes.
These problems could be overcome and reliability could be
increased by setting up the usual social scientific programs
to train the users of an instrument so that it is utilized in

substantially similar ways. Certainly there would be nothing to preclude this with the profile. However, the major thrust of this work is to achieve ways of studying ethnic behavior that *any* teacher who is interested may adapt to his or her existing circumstances. The knowledge a teacher acquires will be limited to her or his own class or school, and it is the teacher who will have to seek ways of checking her or his own observations.

ACTION RESEARCH BY TEACHERS

Generalizations based on the profile must never be considered more than tentative—a set of plausible hypotheses about the way a group behaves. Nevertheless, these tentative generalizations may be used for developing or modifying instructional techniques such as classroom management and lesson planning. Using hypotheses as the basis for classroom activities must mean continual evaluation and revision. Teachers must consciously engage in an effort to evaluate the outcomes against various kinds of criteria; they must be willing to restructure techniques, revise generalizations, and continue collecting ethnic data on a permanent basis.

In effect, the classroom becomes a laboratory of ongoing human experimentation. Of course, in medicine or other applied fields of science, such action research would be unthinkable. Public education, however, is constantly trying things out on students—making decisions that often have far reaching effects on their lives. Teachers are invariably involved in taking actions for which they have little (if any) scientifically demonstrable support. Such actions could be made more sensitive and more effective by being transformed into action research, that is, into teaching activities planned on the basis of tentative generalizations about ethnic behaviors observed.

Clearly, this is a new kind of research, which, although making some use of scientific methods, incorporates a posture of ongoing tentativeness, individual judgments (of teachers), and daily decision-making activities (of teachers) in a way that combines scientific and humanistic research techniques. It is hoped that this rather unique technique will bring more rational analysis of behavior to the schools than is now the case, while still reflecting the fundamentally applicative, qualitative, and changing nature of the teaching enterprise.

An example may help to characterize the type of research being proposed. Cartographers or mapmakers transform the three-dimensional, solid world into a two-dimensional projection. To do so, they use clearly defined, mathematical rules. Whenever these rules are followed for the same location, the same map is produced. Cartographers are engaged in a scientific endeavor. Painters of realistic scenes also transform the three-dimensional world into a two-dimensional image by following a set of shared rules. The rules, however, are not precisely defined and are subject to change because of the artists' personalities or the unique topic being painted. Some of the rules can be shared precisely with other artists, and some are both indefinite and subjective. Painters of realistic scenes are engaged in endeavors similar to the action research proposed here.

THE ETHNIC PROFILE IN PRACTICE

Using the profile does require following systematic procedures by which rational analyses can be achieved. The ethnic profile is used in two distinct phases. The first phase is data collecting, during which entries based on empirical observations are simply placed under the appropriate aspect without any effort at organizing them. The format my students and I used for this phase was that of five colums, placed side by side, one for each aspect, in which empirical observations were jotted down.

Mimeographed sheets of this form were placed in a looseleaf binder so that all our entries, regardless of when they were made, would be together. We tried not to review or even remember preceding entries in an effort to lessen the influence past observations might have on the manner in which our entries were phrased.

ETHNIC PROFILE (for phase one)

Verbal Communication	*Nonverbal Communication*	*Orientation Modes*	*Social Value Patterns*	*Intellectual Modes*

Phase One: Collecting Data

Of course, we tried to make our entries objective descriptions of the activities we observed. This meant trying to avoid the use of adjectives that had other than intersubjectively understood information and modifying, wherever possible, descriptions relative to our own experience. An entry such as, "She smiled kindly" was too subjective; there are any number of ways a person can smile, which can be interpreted as "kindly." "Kindly" in this effort became "broadly, with her lips apart and her teeth very visible." If we were also trying to study our own reactions to behavior, we made some note in square brackets such as [kindly].

Trying to avoid descriptions that reflected our own experiences was quite difficult. For instance, an entry such as, "He talked slowly" was very problematic. How slowly was "slowly?" The only way my students could come to some agreement on such questions was to look for a criterion that they were all familiar with and use the adjective or adverb in relationship to that criterion. With regard to speaking slowly or quickly, we decided to use a television newscaster's rate of speed as our criterion for an average rate of speech. Thus, the term slowly was no longer relative to our own personal experience but to an empirical experience we all shared. Since we hoped to be able to organize our separate observations into a series of generalizations about a group's ethnicity, establishing such external criteria was absolutely necessary. Although externalized criteria diminished individual subjectivity, they did not overcome it. Furthermore, the criteria were established on the basis of agreements of the observers and could not be proven accurate. They were humanistically reached decisions made by a group of action researchers so that they could talk over, with greater clarity, among themselves what they were observing.

Initially, we had difficulty formulating entries based on the *single* behavioral components of complex activities in which many actions occurred simultaneously. We needed to collect single behavioral components and then, by noting the frequency of their occurrence, determine the likelihood of their being ethnically acquired behaviors or behaviors of a personal origin. Since repetition of a behavior by various members of an ethnic group is one basis for generalizing about that group's ethnicity, this requires separating behaviors that occur simultaneously. Of course, people do not split their activities into ethnic and personal behaviors; in the same instance, an individual may exhibit both personal and ethnic behaviors.

A few examples may help to clarify this point. While talking to his teacher, a young boy is chewing gum, pulling at his ear, and jiggling his foot. He is talking in a moderate tone but very quickly (relative to a T.V. newscaster) and is asking a question about something he doesn't understand. Given that these behaviors are likely to happen in less than a minute, more than one observer would be useful. One observer could note the young boy's speech patterns such as pausal behavior and verbal fluency, while a second observer could view his actions while talking to his teacher, making the following set of single entries:

1. While talking to his teacher, a young boy chews gum. (listed under nonverbal communication, diakinesic/ punctuational)
2. While talking to his teacher, a young boy clicks his gum continuously. [Rude] (listed under nonverbal communication, diakinesic/punctuational)

3. While talking to his teacher a young boy jiggles his right foot, keeping the sole of his foot on the floor and moving the heel up and down. (listed under nonverbal communication, diakinesic/punctuational)
4. While talking to his teacher, a young boy pulls at his earlobe with obviousness and regularity but not so hard as to cause him any apparent pain. (listed under nonverbal communication, diakinesic/punctuational)

"While talking to his teacher" specifies, at least partially, the context within which the activity occurs and need not be counted as a single behavioral component. Pulling one's ear and jiggling one's foot are single behavioral components, even if they happen simultaneously. Separating the components and describing each one as independent occurrences enables action researchers to analyze their entries with greater objectivity. For example, suppose foot jiggling is observed only sporadically among the members of an ethnic group, while gum chewing is observed frequently among many members of the group. In drawing up tentative generalizations, it would be reasonable to think of gum chewing as having an ethnic relationship and foot jiggling as being of a personal origin. Then, too, suppose that vigorous gum chewing is observed in a variety of contexts, such as while alone in a library or while walking down the hallway. It might be more reasonable to think of gum chewing as an ethnic orientation mode rather than as a way of communicating. The observer of the young boy placed the word "rude" in brackets after the second entry, which indicated that the observer received a message that seemed to say the young boy had little respect for the teacher. Repeated observations of the same behavior in many contexts would indicate that the observer had ascribed some meaning to the behavior not intended by the young boy. For the observer-teacher, this is a very important kind of realization.

Methodological uncertainty is clearly present in the above four-entry example. Other entries might have been developed such as, "While talking to his teacher, a young boy talks very quickly." The context might have been expanded to indicate whether the teacher was a male or female. The choice of descriptive words could also have been different. Instead of jiggling, "shaking up and down" might have been used and might carry a different meaning. To compensate for these and other uncertainties, as many single component entries as possible should be collected by as many observers as possible during the first phase of profile making.

Phase Two: Analyzing Data

The second phase of the study is that in which entries are analyzed by all observers in a general group discussion or, if there is only one observer, then this phase must be one of reflective review. The purpose of phase two is to determine which entries can be used to establish tentative generalizations and which ought to be held in abeyance until further data is collected and which might then be eliminated as not having sufficient bearing on a group's ethnicity. Phase one continues while phase two is being undertaken as well as after phase two has been suspended. Phase one is conceived as a continuous process of data collection feeding into phase two, which is a periodic assessment of the data collected. The tentative generalizations made during prior phase two periods of assessment are considered with new data collected so that the generalizations too are continually revised.

Sources of Data

There are several different sources for ethnic profile entries:

1. Anecdotal observations
2. Informal observations
3. Formal observations
4. Structured observations
5. Experimental observations.

An anecdotal observation is an experience an individual has

had that he or she feels is interesting or important enough to tell someone else about. For the most part, this is the kind of talk that occurs in lunchroom discussions among teachers about their students. It may also be the kind of incident that newspaper writers might relate about their personal experiences. The anecdote is subjective (though not necessarily unfair) and is likely to contain several unexamined generalizations, which may be used as data inputs during phase one but should not become generalizations for phase two unless other inputs confirm them.

An informal observation is data collected from a published work based on a collection of observations that the author tries to summarize and interpret. Although tending toward the anecdotal, the effort involved in organizing such observations in a purposeful fashion lends more credence to this source. More reflection is likely, and more care is given to details than in the simple anecdote.

A formal observation resembles the informal observation as it is an account prepared in some purposeful fashion for public consumption. It differs in that the effort of the writer is based on her or his *established expertise,* that is, her or his objective descriptions and logical linkages between the facts and the generalizations presented. Since anyone using the ethnic profile would not want to become involved in judging the quality of an expert's performance, any piece written by a recognized authority would qualify as a formal observation.

The structured observation is data collected according to systematically established procedures that can be clearly and empirically described. The ethnic profile does not fully qualify as an instrument of structured observation because of the ambiguities of observing human behavior in natural environmental settings, which were discussed earlier in this chapter. However, within each of the aspects of ethnicity, the development of instruments to achieve structured observations of some component of the category is possible and often desirable. For example, nonverbal kinesic studies are extremely difficult for an action researcher to describe objectively and accurately. An instrument whose format helps a researcher make observations more quickly than written descriptions and with less subjectivity than is normally found in nonverbal descriptions is likely to contribute to the general quality of nonverbal observations. Such an instrument is proposed in Appendix A.

The experimental observation has all the characteristics of the structured observation, but, in addition, implies some control over the conditions in the situation being observed. For example, students of similar socioeconomic circumstances and similar educational aspirations and I.Q. test scores are administered a series of tests. If two or three known ethnic groups are participants in the experiment, test score differences may be related to diverse ethnic backgrounds since socioeconomic and other factors have been controlled. Extreme caution must be taken in such controlled experiments for there are almost always many more factors influencing human behavior than can possibly be controlled experimentally.

In developing an ethnic profile, all kinds of data dources need to be used. While structured and experimental observations may yield more reliably objective data, they are often not as appropriate for seeking out latent social value patterns as the more casual anecdotes and informal observations. Structured observations may be very useful in expanding the objective data input of an aspect of ethnicity, but the formal observation may be equally useful in obtaining a global view of a group's ethnic traits. In sum, the full range of available kinds of data sources needs to be employed in the study of ethnicity.

The development of ethnic profiles does not require a large number of action researchers—one willing teacher is enough to start. Nor is a high level of expertise an absolute requirement. It is, of course, hoped that as the study of a group progresses, single entries will be made with increased objectivity and that structured and experimental observations will be undertaken. It is further hoped that all the subcategories of the five aspects will eventually contain numerous entries supporting the description of an ethnic group. But none of this is necessary to start. Action researchers do what is within their means to do.

Initially my students and I developed ethnic profiles based on only three types of data sources: anecdotes and informal and formal observations. These were the sources most readily available to us and to the teachers who cooperated with our studies. We were able to begin to use these with relatively little preparation, though with much care and humility. While not fully sufficient, these data sources can be adopted by a group of teachers in a school in the initial development of ethnic profiles. I had only an eight-month period with each group of student teachers and, since I believed that a concerted effort to describe systematically the attributes of an ethnic group increases observers' sensitivities to the group they are observing,[1] I was anxious for my students to begin their observations as soon as possible. Their direct observations were anecdotal inputs, and their library research was treated as either informal or formal observations. Initially the subcategories of the five aspects were used as guides for our observations but not as subheadings for data retrieval purposes; we placed our entries directly into the major aspects of ethnicity. The subcategories only proved useful for retrieval as the number of entries increased.

The presentation of all these technical considerations may be somewhat confusing as was the case for some of my students. For several days we discussed examples of the three sources of data that we were going to use to develop profiles. A few examples and the derivation of single behavioral components used as entries for the ethnic profile during phase one follow to clarify the preceding discussion.

EXAMPLES OF ANECDOTAL OBSERVATIONS

Anecdote 1

This happened in the summer of 1971 while I was preparing for the Chicago Schools Project. I was sitting in a waffle house in Lincoln, Nebraska, with a friend; my back was to most of the dining room.

We were having a rather pleasant, aimless conversation when my friend interrupted: "I just can't keep my eyes off a white haired lady sitting in the middle of the room. She's got six kids with her—not one of them over eight or nine—and she's having a full fledged discussion with each one of them about what they want to eat." The description hit a chord of memory inside me. I had been brought up by a Jewish grandmother, and I remembered vividly our many discussions over what I would eat.

We both started to listen to the white haired lady, though all we could see was her back and sometimes the side of her cheek: "Are you sure, honey, that's what you want? Remember, you left your pancakes yesterday? Why don't you try some eggs or a waffle?" She turned to another child: "Do you think you can eat those pancakes without ruining your dress? Maybe you should get something else?" We could not hear the children's responses, but her conversation was a running one, filled with questions for the children's consideration.

I turned to my friend and said, "I bet she's Jewish!" He naturally was skeptical, but I insisted, "The way she's acting with those kids is so much like the way my grandma used to act with me . . ." Curiosity got the better of my inhibitions, and I was on the verge of going over to her and asking whether she were Jewish, when she got up from the table. "I'll be right back," she said, "Tell the waitress what you want." She headed for the rest room. Not only did her features confirm my hypothesis about her Jewishness, but she was wearing a star of David around her neck. My friend smiled, but he really didn't understand why I had been so sure. Nor do I completely understand, for much of my reaction was a kind of emotional response to a way of acting that had been a part of my childhood but that I had not known for many years.

Analysis

On the basis of this brief anecdote, several classifiable statements of behavior and related inference may be made about Jews living in Lincoln, Nebraska, as well as about Jews living in New York, where I spent most of my childhood.

American Jew, Lincoln, Nebraska, and
New York City Background

1. In a restaurant and during a conversation between an adult woman and children about eight-nine years old, the woman poses numerous questions about what each child wants to eat.
2. In a restaurant and during a conversation between an adult woman and children about eight-nine years old, the woman waits for each child to make a decision about what he or she wants and seems to be willing to order accordingly.
3. In posing many questions about the choice of food to eight-nine-year-old children, the adult woman asks each youngster to reflect upon the wiseness of his or her choice (i.e., Are you sure . . . ? Maybe you should . . . ?)
4. A group of young children (six) between the ages of eight and nine are expected to behave well enough in a restaurant to be left alone briefly without anyone watching them.
5. When left alone in a restaurant, a group of young children (six) between the ages of eight and nine are expected to order for themselves if necessary.

Statement one is easily placed as an exploratory-inquiry discussion mode under the verbal aspect of ethnicity. Statement two might be similarly placed, but because of its emphasis on the expected decision, must also definitely be included as an entry for social value patterns. This seems to be a latent, individually oriented pattern reflecting desirable, preferred behavior. Whether it is secondary or dominant must await many more entries and a phase two analysis. An area of study not mentioned in Chapter VIII's analysis of social value patterns might eventually need to be developed involving patterns of behavior in public places such as at restaurants and meetings. In the initial stages, however, specification of areas of behavioral patterns should not occur until the phase two review of inputs collected during phase one has been undertaken several times. In this way, the categories developed (e.g., delinquency pattern, family patterns, and so on) will be based on an analysis of observed behaviors.

Statement three, which encourages considering the consequences of and alternatives to decisions made, would be best placed under intellectual modes, ways of confronting problems, and is an example of abstract reasoning as related to ethnic approaches to learning. Statements four and five are considered social value pattern entries. As more entries are collected, statements two, four, and five might become inputs in the manifest-latent continuum. Such a development, however, would need to await at least the first phase two review and generalization period.

Anecdote 2

While I was conducting a graduate workshop for improving teaching to ethnically different groups, two students could not come at the established hour, and I agreed to have classes with them when their schedules would permit. Both were women between their late twenties and early thirties. One was of Swedish-American background and had spent the major part of her life in rural Illinois. The other was of Jewish-American heritage and had grown up in a middle-class area of Chicago.

This particular day I was trying to explain how a nonverbal observation checklist could be used (see Appendix A). While not complicated, the instrument involves a glossary of symbols for describing body movements. The graduate student of Jewish-American background had scheduled her class with me an hour before the other woman was to come. For nearly the entire hour she pummeled me with questions about every aspect of the instrument. I had the feeling I was being challenged. I no sooner finished a statement and was on the verge of developing its logical consequence, when she would pop in with questions, some of which were really unnecessary, though not at all unintelligent. This behavior made me reflect on my own ways of learning in a traditional teacher-learner situation. I had to recognize that though the habit had diminished considerably with age, I still tended to ask a lot of questions when I was being taught something new. Furthermore, I recalled, with an astounding frequency those students who asked the most questions (many inane, many insightful) in my classes were of Jewish background. This, of course, was an unexamined stereotype.

I decided to do some empirical investigating. I undertook to teach the same non-verbal observation checklist to the second woman in a manner as similar to the previous lesson as my memory would permit. My objective was to compare the number of questions the woman of Swedish-American origin would ask with the number asked by the student of Jewish-American origin. Since the experiment grew unexpectedly out of casual circumstances, I had neither an accurate accounting of the number of questions that had actually been asked by my Jewish student nor a sufficient number of subjects upon which to make comparisons. Still, I thought, the outcome could be used as input for an ethnic profile. If the outcome were not substantiated by a number of other observations, it would simply be eliminated from the ethnic profile as a personality trait. Generalizations and hypotheses should never be derived from one observations or on the basis of one informant's perceptions.

The results of my off-the-cuff experiment were so clear that counting the number of questions was, in this instance, completely unnecessary. The student of Swedish-American background asked no questions whatsoever while I was explaining the checklist. She did shake her head up and down a good deal of the time. She also "uh-huhed" intermittently while looking straight at me. At the end of my explanation, she asked for several examples in a manner in which she summarized what I had said as well as asked me how to translate it into something practical. I realized, upon reflection, that I could not remember the nonverbal forms used by the Jewish student, perhaps because I was so involved in responding to her numerous questions.

Analysis

On the basis of this brief anecdote of an informal experiment, several entries for the ethnic profile may be made about American Jews of Chicago background and Swedish Americans of rural Illinois background.

American Jew of Chicago Background

1. While learning something new in a one-to-one student-teacher relationship, a young woman student asks many questions during the teacher's explanation.
2. While learning something new in a one-to-one student-teacher relationship, a young woman student asks sets of questions often not clearly connected with the particular aspect of learning at hand. [antagonistically challenging]

Swedish-American, Illinois, Rural Background

3. While learning something new in a one-to-one student-teacher relationship, a young woman student asks no questions during the teachers explanation.
4. While learning something new in a one-to-one student-teacher relationship, a young woman student asks questions that summarize what has been said after the teacher's explanation has been completed.
5. During a one-to-one student-teacher relationship, a young woman student shakes her head up and down. [indicating understanding]
6. During a one-to-one student-teacher relationship, a young woman student vocalizes "uh-huh" intermittently. [indicating understanding]
7. During a one-to-one student-teacher relationship, a young woman student looks directly at her teacher during the explanation. [indicating understanding]

It cannot be emphasized enough that the behaviors listed above, all taken from a single incident, are *unacceptable* as the basis for generalizations about ethnic groups. As contributions to a global view and as clues for possible generalizations, they are useful. Each of the statements could reflect scholastic ethnicity or unique personality traits as well ethnic background. Only numerous observations from a wide variety of sources (and, when possible, by observers of diverse ethnic backgrounds) can help determine the relatedness of an observation to a group's ethnicity.

Statements one, two, three, and four would be classified under intellectual modes as approaches to learning and behavior during new learning. Statements five and seven describe nonverbal communication activities (kinesics). Statement six, referring to the use of "uh-huh," would be placed under verbal denotative language rules describing semantic meaning.

A statement can be placed under more than one ethnic aspect if it actually reflects more than one function. Thus, all the statements regarding questioning could be placed under discussion modes of verbal communication, since questioning has simultaneous importance for learning styles as well as for discussion modes. If a statement can be subdivided into behavioral components that distinguish their importance for the two categories, this should, of course, be done. However, asking a question about something being learned may reflect, simultaneously, a way of learning and a way of relating in discussion. In such an instance, the same entry would need to be made in two categories.

EXAMPLES OF INFORMAL OBSERVATIONS

Unlike anecdotes, which are usually about firsthand, unplanned experiences, informal observations are provided by professional writers who earn their living observing and then summarizing and interpreting their observations. Such professionals have been divided into two groups: those who base their writings (including scripts for television and the like) on an assortment of casual sources and observations, and those who attempt to achieve some level of objective description and defensible analysis. The informal observations of the first group are usually found in the occasional articles of newspapers and magazines, in novels, and hour-long television programs. The more formal observations of the latter group are likely to belong to a growing body of papers written by professional social scientists without the strict use of structured and experimental observations. Articles of this sort are generally found in widely read but specialized journals such as *Society, Psychology Today,* and *Sceptic.*

Examples of informal and formal observations that demonstrate the development of phase one data follow. Because of the limitations of space, excerpts rather than complete works are presented, even though the act of choosing excerpts introduces the possibility of increasing subjectivity. The development of a sample phase one profile is useful primarily in clarifying how an ongoing ethnic profile can be achieved and put into use by public school teachers.

Informal Excerpt 1

There is a saying that Jews like to quote, which is that "if you have six Jews in a room, you'll have nine different opinions." Perhaps this is because in the old days, in the ghettos of Russia and Poland and Central Europe, where Jews were oppressed and confined and forced inward on one another, required to find their resources in one another, treated as "outsiders" wherever they went, argument—for the sheer joy and edification of it, the mental limbering up that good argument involves—became a pastime, a diversion, and escape from life's vicissitudes, even an art form. Jewish women are good arguers, they cultivate strong opinions, and they learn how to express and defend them. It makes them smart.[2]

Analysis

While the writer, Stephen Birmingham, has overlooked other possible reasons for the argumentative ways of the Jews, such as the great honor given to considering the meaning of the Old

Testament, this does not undermine the usefulness of the article as one of the numerous sources for entries into phase one. Of course, this assumes using many kinds of informal observations by observers of widely differing backgrounds and views.

General American Jew

1. Jews generally hold widely divergent opinions even when in small groups. Note: This entry is based on the quote, "Six Jews in a room, you'll have nine different opinions."
2. Jews enjoy arguing.
3. A "good" argument is considered a diversion and escape from life's vicissitudes.
4. A "good" argument may be thought of as an art form.
5. Jewish women cultivate strong opinions.
6. Jewish women learn how to express and defend themselves in arguments.

Clearly, some of the above statements are laden with obscure descriptions such as "good" and "escape from life's vicissitudes." While such usage should be avoided whenever teachers themselves engage in developing entries, their elimination by those collecting data from published sources would risk not only the loss of information but the injection of their own biases by tinkering with the biases of others. For the sake of objectivity, numerous diverse sources must be used without modifying what might otherwise be considered obscure terms.

Statements one, two, three, and four are all social value patterns describing desirable behavior at the dominant, manifest, and individually oriented levels. In other words, the Jew is widely expected to hold independent opinions, and this is considered desirable. It may also be considered a prized behavior (rather than having moral value). Of course, other entries may negate the choice of some of these descriptors, but that kind of determination can only be made after numerous entries have been collected and the phase two stage of developing an ethnic profile has been undertaken. Statements one, two, and four also carry some import for discussion modes and might be usefully included under the ethnic aspect of verbal communication. Statements five and six deal with intellectual modes, with five emphasizing qualities of verbal fluency and six referring to the development of verbal fluency in specific activities.

Informal Excerpt 2

The following comments were made by Italians employed in various aspects of American tourism:

> There is another thing—I don't know if it's the fact of being American—they have very little awareness of the European situation. Americans criticize a lot, just to criticize—everything: politics, the economy, customs. And they often criticize without knowing the situation.

> Many Americans make themselves disagreeable just because of all the books that they have. For example, the Fielding book should be burned, because of its insulting "be-careful-those-foreigners-will-rob-you" warnings.

> The trouble is that tourists take it (Fielding book) literally. They leave America with the Fielding book, and if they don't find somebody who can explain things to them, they will go on believing the book forever, as if it were the Bible.

> .. they also don't speak English correctly as they should. With everybody, everybody, they ask first, "Do you speak English?" Yes, I do, and they speak—if they're from the North or the South—with a dialect.

> They are quite lazy about the language (Italian). You know, just familiar expressions—*buon giorno, ciao, arriverderci,* just to make a show.[3]

Analysis

The above excerpt provides possibilities for investigating a general American white ethnicity. It is reasoned that, for the most part, American travelers to Europe are viewed as a cohesive group, and stereotypes regarding the way Americans act as a whole are more likely to arise among foreign people than among Americans themselves. Some of these stereotypes might be accurate reflections of American ethnic behaviors; some may be overgeneralizations. In any case, the impressions foreigners have of American travelers seem a promising source for developing an initial profile of general American white ethnicity.

General White American

1. When traveling abroad, Americans criticize indiscriminately often without knowing the situation.
2. When traveling abroad, Americans take *Fielding's Guide* literally and believe everything in it.
3. When traveling abroad, Americans believe Fielding's " 'be-careful-those-foreigners-will-rob-you' warnings."
4. When traveling abroad, Americans speak dialects (rather than Standard English).
5. When traveling abroad, Americans are lazy about learning Italian.

Statement one is simultaneously an entry for discussion modes of the controversial type and of intellectual skills emphasizing verbal fluency in the context of criticism. The value and credence that Americans seem to have in *Fielding's Guide* places statements two and three under the aspect of social value patterns. In particular, statement three seems to refer to buying patterns of a dominant, group oriented, manifest nature. Statement two, the credence placed on the written word, seems to reflect an educational pattern that is also dominant, group oriented, and manifest in nature (at least within the context of the excerpt). Statement four is clearly a statement regarding rules of verbal communication, i.e., the rules of a dialect, not of Standard English, are used. Statement five, which may at first glance seem to be classifiable under verbal communication, actually represents an American attitude toward acquiring a particular intellectual skill and thus belongs under verbal fluency in the context of a foreign language. At this point, direct overlap with an educational social value pattern might be thought to exist. However, educational patterns imply some formalization, if only of the attitudes held toward books. Saying even a few simple words in a foreign tongue while abroad really refers to a general attitude held about a particular intellectual skill independently of formal education.

EXAMPLES OF FORMAL OBSERVATIONS

Formal Excerpt 1

In one ingeniously conceived study the investigator compared two groups of boys from a Brooklyn Jewish neighborhood. Though the boys live close to one another and are of the same middle-class composition, their ethnic backgrounds differ historically. One is Ashkenazi, the European Jew whose tradition emphasizes the importance of scholarship and learning; the other is Sephardic, whose tradition puts stress on commercial and financial success. When the average I.Q.'s of the groups on entering school are compared, one finds a substantial and significant difference. The families representing the Ashkenazi tradition apparently provide the kind of environment in which verbal performance is rewarded and in which the child is urged to achieve in that area, enabling him to do much better on the I.Q. test.[4]

Analysis

American Jew, New York City Background

1. American Jews of Ashkenazi tradition, living in the New York City area, perform well on I.Q. tests as measured by criteria established in the public schools.
2. American Jews of Ashkenazi tradition, living in the New York City area, perform well in verbal skills according to standards set in the public schools
3. American Jews of Sephardic tradition, living in the New

York City area, do not perform as well verbally as do Ashkenazi Jews living in the same area, as measured by criteria established in the public schools.

5. The traditions of Ashkenazi Jews stress scholarship and learning.
6. The traditions of Sephardic Jews stress commercial and financial success.

Statements one through four clearly refer to the intellectual abilities of verbal fluency and the ethnic emphasis placed on them. Statements one and four further specify the context as the standard I.Q. tests. Statements five and six can also be placed in the aspect of intellectual modes under typical contexts and activities, i.e., Sephardic Jews exercise their intellectual abilities in one set of topics, the Ashkenazi in another. These latter two statements are equally relevant to social value patterns, but it must be remembered that they are uninvestigated generalizations derived from a single formal observation. Their entry into phase one of the profile indicates merely tentative consideration that such generalizations might be sustained in future observations.

Formal Excerpt 2

In the large corporation, just as in the Army, the executive feels a need for highly visible signs of his authority, even though he feels a need simultaneously to act out the American Creed by showing what a nice, regular fellow he is.

First, there is the physical problem of assigning office space. This is often done by rule. Crown Zellerback Corporation, in planning its move to a new twenty-story building, has arranged walls so that offices for executives of equal rank can "all be built to within a square inch of one another in size." In a typical corporation, the head of the hierarchy assigned to a floor gets the corner office with the nicest view and the offices of his subordinates branch out from his corner in descending order of rank. Physical closeness to the center of power is considered evidence of status; and nobody wants to be put out "in left field."[5]

Analysis

General White American

1. In the large corporation, the size of an office is indicative of an excutive's authority in the corporation, i.e., the larger the office, the greater the authority and vice versa.
2. In the large corporation, the most authoritative executive assigned to a floor will have a corner office with the nicest [criteria for determining "nice" unknown] view.
3. In the large corporation, the physical closeness of an executive's office to the floor's most important executive indicates more status, while greater distance from the most important executive indicates less status.
4. In the large corporation, executives feel the need for symbols of their authority.
5. In the large corporation, executives want to show they are "nice, regular" fellows. [criteria unknown]

The first three statements refer to the meaning of spatial arrangements and would be placed in the proxemics category of nonverbal communication. Statements four and five refer to the value executives place on the images of themselves, which they project to others in the corporation, and would be classified under social value patterns as described by Packard. They are group oriented, dominant, but somewhat latent kinds of behavior.

A SAMPLE PHASE ONE PROFILE

Here is an initial profile at the phase one stage of data collection developed for Jewish Americans on the bases of the preceding anecdotes, informal excerpts, and formal excerpts. It is only a sample formed with a very limited number of inputs to exemplify the methodology being proposed to teachers for in-

SAMPLE PROFILE (BEGINNING PHASE ONE) JEWISH AMERICAN

Verbal Communication	Nonverbal Communication	Orientation Modes	Social Value Patterns	Intellectual Modes
1. In a restaurant and during a conversation between an adult woman and children about eight and nine years old, a woman poses numerous questions about what each child wants to eat. (Nebraska/New York City) 2. In a restaurant and during a conversation between an adult and children about			1. In a restaurant and during a conversation between an adult and children about eight and nine years old, a woman waits for each child to make a decision about what he or she wants and seems to be willing to order accordingly. (Nebraska/New York City) 2. A group of young children (six) between the ages of eight and nine are expected to behave well enough in a restaurant to be left alone briefly without anyone at all watching them. (Nebraska/New York City) 3. When left alone in a restaurant, a group of young children (six) between the ages of eight and nine are	1. In posing many questions about the choice of food to eight-and nine-year-old children, the adult woman will ask the youngster to reflect upon the wiseness of his choice. (i.e., Are you sure ...? Maybe you should ...? etc.) (Nebraska/New York City) 2. While learning something new in a one-to-one student-teacher relationship, a young woman student will ask many questions during the teacher's explanation. (Chicago) 3. While learning something new in a one-to-one student-teacher relationship, a young woman student will ask sets of questions often not clearly connected with the particular aspect of learning at hand. (Chicago) *Informal **Formal Omission of asterisk indicates ancedote

SAMPLE PROFILE (BEGINNING PHASE ONE) JEWISH AMERICAN

Verbal Communication	Nonverbal Communication	Orientation Modes	Social Value Patterns	Intellectual Modes
eight and nine years old, the woman waits for each child to make a decision about what he or she wants and seems to be willing to order accordingly. (Nebraska/New York City) 3. Jews generally hold widely divergent opinions even when in small groups.* 4. Jews enjoy arguing.*			expected to order for themselves if necessary. (Nebraska/New York City) 4. Jews generally hold widely divergent opinions even when in small groups.* 5. Jews enjoy arguing.* 6. A "good" argument is considered a diversion and escape from life's vicissitudes.* 7. A "good" argument may be thought of as an art form.*	4. Jewish women cultivate strong opinions.* 5. Jewish women learn how to express and defend themselves in arguments.* 6. American Jews of Ashkenazi tradition living in the New York City area perform well on I.Q. tests as measured by criteria established in the public schools.** 7. American Jews of Ashkenazi tradition, living in the New York City area, perform well in verbal skills according to standards set in the public schools.** 8. American Jews of Sephardic tradition, living in the New York City area, do not perform as well verbally as do Ashkenazi Jews living in the same area, according to standards set in the public schools. *Informal **Formal Omission of asterisk indicates ancedote

SAMPLE PROFILE (BEGINNING PHASE ONE) JEWISH AMERICAN

Verbal Communication	Nonverbal Communication	Orientation Modes	Social Value Patterns	Intellectual Modes
5. A "good" argument may be thought of as an art form.*			8. The traditions of Ashkenazi Jews stress scholarship and learning.** 9. The traditions of Sephardic Jews stress commercial and financial success.**	9. American Jews of Sephardic tradition, living in the New York City area, do not perform as well on I.Q. tests as do Ashkenazi Jews living in the same area, as measured by criteria established in the public schools.** 10. The tradition of Ashkenazi Jews stress scholarship and learning.** 11. The traditions of Sephardic Jews stress commercial and financial success.**

*Informal
**Formal
Omission of asterisk indicates ancedote

creasing their understanding of diverse ethnic groups. This data collection phase will increase its potential to help teachers achieve greater ethnic insights as the number of observers and observations increase.

During the earliest period of phase one, the number of entries made in the profile will be relatively few, and the five major aspects of ethnicity will be sufficient for classifying the entries. However, as the numbers increase, there will be a need to use the subcategories outlined at the end of Chapters III through VIII. These subcategories will assist observers to retrieve their data when they are needed during the period of tentative generalizations (phase two). It must again be noted that the subcategories help shape the way information will be looked for in describing each aspect of ethnicity. Because a subcategory of touching (haptics) has been developed under nonverbal communication, understanding of this behavior is more likely achieved than if it were included by implication under the diakenesic system or as a symbol of some kind.

Similarly, in the preceding sample profile no entries were made for either nonverbal communication or orientation modes. A good action researcher would therefore begin to seek data in these areas. Researchers need to question the usefulness and validity of the categories continually, making modifications they believe will lead toward greater effectiveness of the profile as a data collecting and retrieving instrument. The profile, as it stands now, is a heuristic *tour de force* that my students and I developed because we deeply felt the need for such an instrument. I sincerely hope it will be improved as it continues to be used.

In the preceding sample, each entry is followed by the geographic location, if known, and by an indication of its source. No asterisk signifies an anecdote; one asterisk signifies an informal observation, two asterisks signify a formal observation; if a structured observation were used, three asterisks could represent this source, while four asterisks could indicate an experimental observation. If a teacher were also trying to monitor her or his own reaction to direct observations (anecdotes in all probability, though structured and experimental observations are possible), brackets with brief comments of reaction could also be placed after an entry.

Noting the kinds of sources used is a way of monitoring whether variety has been employed in gathering data. Have books, articles, direct observation, or experiments been used? This is important if objectivity is to be achieved. Noting the geographic location helps teachers determine whether a generalization about an ethnic group is or is not supported locally. What may be true in one area of the country about an ethnic group may not apply to that same ethnic group in another region.

Another point needs to be made about the uses of the sub-categories or outlines of the five aspects of ethnicity. Just as a topographic map of a mountainous, rugged area will use many descriptors that are quite different from those used in a map of a flat plains area, the aspects have been described in different ways. There are, of course, underlying similarities based on the fact that all the behaviors to be included under any of the aspects must fit the given definition of ethnicity. However, the outline for nonverbal behavior is quite different from the outline for social value patterns. In nonverbal behavior, it is feasible to distinguish as separate entities the different non-verbal patterns used in communication even if these occur simultaneously. I can note without undue difficulty the distances people are sitting from each other as distinct from the way they are smiling or moving their eyes; I can even try to observe how often a proxemic and kinesic behavior can be found together under similar circumstances. The subcategories are very useful in organizing data for retrieval because the same kind of assumptions underlie their formation, i. e., that nonverbal physical phenomena in human behavior communicate meaning. On the other hand, social value patterns have basically different kinds of phenomena interacting with each other to produce an ethnic social pattern. There are things people do as members of their group, which can be empirically described, that interact with the beliefs and values people hold about the things they do, which cannot be empirically described.

Notations regarding socioeconomic class have been omitted, even though this is usually a major factor in the classification of behavior. I take responsibility for the omission. I have found that the strongly prejudicial nature of connotations associated with class undermine the ability of observers to be objective. Observers who ask themselves under which category an observed behavior should be listed are more objective about what they are watching than those who merely react to a behavior spontaneously. Reactions, however, to socioeconomic class seem to have been learned at such an early age that gaining full control over them is somewhat problematic, even with the use of the profile.

I became reasonably convinced of this during the second term my students and I spent in the Chicago public schools. My students, three of whom were black, had been trying to familiarize themselves with the categories of the ethnic profile. They had spent a week studying ethnic traits of lower-class blacks living in large urban centers (Chicago, St. Louis, and Indianapolis). Their source materials were tapes made of individuals involved in the study of black ethnic traits. It soon became obvious to me that the three black students were becoming increasingly uncomfortable. As middle-class blacks, they clearly resented some of the traits being attributed to poor, urban blacks, which were considered negative and not representative of educated, well-to-do blacks.

At this point, I felt it was important to examine how objective any of these nineteen college students, mostly white, mostly middle class, could be when they were knowingly dealing with a lower-class group. I noted to my students that most of us had had far less experience with lower-class blacks than we had had with lower-class whites; therefore, it seemed reasonable to try to develop a profile for lower-class whites. Since there was only a limited time for the development of this profile, I suggested that each student try to develop a profile from her or his own memory. My students resisted the assignment, feeling very uncomfortable about making a list of their stereotypes. My response was that they had to deal with their own stereotypes and the stereotypes they remembered most readily might be an excellent place to start. With the exception of the negative connotations implicit in the term stereotype, there were no instructions of either a positive or negative nature given regarding the kinds of entries to be made on the ethnic profile sheet.

The results I received from their efforts was startling. Not one entry in the sixteen profiles turned in by the white members of the project was of a favorable nature. The tenor of the entries went something like this: sweaty; beer drinking; women wear too much make-up; greater emphasis on money; individuals of this class consider life as a day-to-day situation; settle differences physically (both men and women); as a rule, a member of this class will work his way up to the fourth grade and either stagnate, push himself further, or quit for a variety of reasons; and talks in "de's," "dems," and "do's." Of all the sixteen white college seniors involved in the project (and they were all volunteers), not one thought to develop an entry such as: realistic view of career prospects; very open and frank in their relationship with others; or dependable laborers. I did not ask the black students to submit their profile unless they wished to do so. They were obviously relieved, and I never saw their entries.

Clearly, the ethnic profiles concerning lower-class whites my students developed from what they recalled were not, nor were they ever intended to be, very revealing about lower-class whites. They were, however, very indicative of the permeating effects that a social concept such as class can have on the individuals' abilities to report their observations objectively.

I am not suggesting that socioeconomic class be ignored during the phases of an ethnic profile's development, but rather that it be delayed as a consideration until phase two when generalizations and possible explanations for entries revealing significant differences in behavioral patterns are needed. I further suggest that it be taken into account only after such considerations as geographic and sex differences have been investigated. By delaying consideration of socioeconomic factors, I believe increased objectivity on the part of observers can be achieved.

FOOTNOTES

[1] No controlled study of this hypothesis has been made although my personal experience seems to confirm its truth.

[2] Stephen Birmingham, "What Makes Jewish Women So Darn Smart," *New Woman,* Vol. II, No. 1, June/July 1972, pp. 80-81 & 98.

[3] Stuart Troup, "When the European Trip Is Over, What Impressions Have Americans Left Behind?" *The New York Times,* Sunday, May 14, 1972, Section 10, p. 1 & 24.

[4] Harry L. Miller and Roger R. Woock, *Social Foundations of Urban Education* (Hinsdale, Ill.: Dryden Press, 1970) p. 157.

[5] Vance Packard, *The Status Seekers* (New York: Pocket Cardinal ed, 1961), p. 104.

CHAPTER X

Phase II and Then What?

I managed to pull together, unfunded by anything but the grit and determination to work with the ideas that had grown from several years of study, a project for student teachers involving twelve Chicago inner-city schools. My students at the University of Illinois in Champaign were mostly of suburban or rural Midwestern backgrounds who had grown up in middle-class socioeconomic circumstances. This was true of the three black women included among the twenty-one participants. (Eventually, two dropped out.)

Among the various methods we explored for developing ethnic profiles was an arrangement in which eleven student teachers, including the three blacks, each located in a separate school, initiated a phase one profile for black Americans of high school age. Because they were all teaching during the eight weeks allocated to this initial period of data collection, only an hour a day was set aside as a planned observation period. However, since all the data collected was considered anecdotal in nature, entries could be made on the basis of classroom experiences occurring outside the allocated hour.

At the end of the eight-week period, the eleven observers met to compare their entries and determine whether any of them might qualify as tentative generalizations in an initial phase two ethnic profile. Total agreement among the participants regarding generalizations of single behavioral components was noted by placing the symbol A-11 in parenthesis immediately following an entry; disagreement was noted by the symbol D, with the tally *for* and *against* immediately following the entry (example:

D-5-6 = five for and six against). In no instance was a generalization accepted for inclusion without at least four separate observations supporting such an entry.

The results of these descriptive efforts follow. I recognize that several inputs are not as careful in the objective use of adjectives and adverbs as is possible. Descriptions such as "proud" and "mechanically competent" carry a high degree of subjective judgment with them and give cause for extreme caution. Nevertheless, the fact that eleven observers (or even four in a few cases) located in different schools made observations that were so similar that they could agree on a single generalization cannot be dismissed because of possible subjective biases in the wording of that generalization.

Nevertheless, some of the classification of entries are really questionable. For instance, entry #5 under Orientation Modes might also have been considered an entry under Nonverbal Communication, proxemics. As a teacher, I feel bound to at least point out the doubts I have about the classification of this entry. But as an action researcher intending to engage in a multiplicity of observations over a long period of time, I know I will encounter a goodly number of entries difficult to classify. Unless they become a major portion of all entries, they will probably pose no real interference with the retrieval function of the profiles. Should the number of doubtfully classified entries become a major characteristic of a profile, it would mean that some revision of the profile itself is in order.

As the accompanying profile shows, we achieved a set of tentative generalizations about the way inner-city black high school students in Chicago communicate verbally and nonverbally, orient themselves, reflect the social value patterns of their group, and perform in intellectual endeavors. So what? If, as teachers, we did not make the conscious effort to modify—at least tentatively—our instructional and classroom behaviors, we would have engaged in one more esoteric exercises, soon to be forgotten in the flood of fads. We needed to hypothesize about the best ways to act if our generalizations were true for a

PHASE TWO ETHNIC PROFILE: BLACK AMERICAN (HIGH SCHOOL STUDENTS CHICAGO)

Nonverbal Communication	Orientation Modes	Verbal Communication	Social Value Patterns	Intellectual Modes
High school males often walk with a proud gait that combines a bouncy step with shuffling and is called the "pimp walk." (A-11) (Chicago) 2. To indicate agreement, two high school males often slap their palms together, using one or both hands, and then take a step backwards away from each other. (A-11) (Chicago) 3. To greet each other, high school males slap their palms together, using one or both hands, and then take a step backwards away from each other. (A-11) (Chi-	1. Among high school students there is a decided preference for sitting at the center desk of the room. (A-11) (Chicago) 2. High school students do not hurry for any school-related reason whatsoever. (A-11) (Chicago) 3. Among high school students, there is a very high rate of lateness to class. (A-11) (Chicago)	1. The use of "mama" is preferred to "mother." (A-11) (Chicago) 2. High school students have difficulty reading aloud literature that has dialogues in black dialect. (A-11) (Chicago) 3. In an argument, high school male students go out of their way to have the last word over the female. (A-11) (Chicago) 4. There was a lot of very audible laughing in the group conversation of high school students. (A-11) (Chicago) 5. High school students dislike having their own names mispronounced. (A-11) (Chicago) 6. High school students	1. High school students have an active dislike for being categorized. (A-11) (Chicago) 2. It is usual for high school students to say they would do anything for money, but their actions do not bear this verbalization out. (A-11) (Chicago) 3. There is a strong tendency for high school students to help each other in class. (A-11) (Chicago) 4. A motto of high school students seems to be: "Do whatever you can get away with." (A-11) (Chicago) 5. Horoscopes are very popular among high	1. High school students are not mechanically competent. (D-6-5) 2. Thinking in abstractions is difficult for high school students. (A-11) (Chicago) 3. High school students remember the complete words to a surprising number of popular songs. (A-11) (Chicago) 4. In learning something new, high school students vocalize a great deal. (A-11) (Chicago) 5. High school students are desirous of performing. (A-11) (Chicago) 6. There seems to be little correlation in high school students between the amount of home-

Nonverbal Communication	Orientation Modes	Verbal Communication	Social Value Patterns	Intellectual Modes
cago) 4. When the teacher approached high school students, they would back away. (A-11) (Chicago) 5. High school males rarely stand straight; they usually lean. (A-11) (Chicago) 6. High school students who do not do well in school prefer to sit at the very back of the room. (A-11) (Chicago) 7. High school males touch females, often holding them by the forearm, in order to get their attention. (A-11) (Chicago) 8. High school females place either one or both	4. If a high school student makes a mistake, he or she tears up the sheet and starts all over again. (D-6-5) (Chicago) 5. High school students perceived the classroom as an area for performance in the theatrical sense. (D-4-7) (Chicago) 6. Many high school male students sit and play "boogies" on a pretend	only approximate the pronunciation of a teacher's name. (A-11) (Chicago) 7. Everything high school students say is loud. (D-4-7) (Chicago) 8. High school students refuse to repeat anything once they have said it. (A-11) (Chicago) 9. High school students do not say "please" and "thank you." (D-10-1) (Chicago) 10. Among high school students, there is a noticeably high frequency of the term, "good luck." (A-11) (Chicago) 11. Ts and ds are not sounded by high school	school students. (A-11) (Chicago) 6. It is desirable, though often not possible, for high school male students to wear expensive, flashy clothes. (A-11) (Chicago) 7. While high school students seem to be very militant in conversation, they take few positions against anything. (A-11) (Chicago) 8. Many high school males express the desire to become "pimps." (D-9-2) (Chicago) 9. Education is less important than money. (A-11) (Chicago) 10. Immediate occurrences are the most im-	work accomplished at home and classroom learning. (D-7-4) (Chicago) 7. High school students are frequently able to spell words orally but not in writing. (D-5-6) (Chicago) 8. When high school students reach a certain point of frustration in learning something, they do not work harder to "get" it. (D-9-2) (Chicago) 9. The ability to be humorous among high school students is well developed. (D-10-1) (Chicago) 10. High school students exhibit a great deal of

PHASE TWO ETHNIC PROFILE: BLACK AMERICAN (HIGH SCHOOL STUDENTS CHICAGO)

Nonverbal Communication	Orientation Modes	Verbal Communication	Social Value Patterns	Intellectual Modes
hands on their hips when they are angry. (A-11) (Chicago)	piano continually even when no one is apparently paying any attention to them. (A-11) (Chicago)	students. (A-11) (Chicago)	portant; today is more important than next week. (A-11) (Chicago)	curiosity. (D-10-1) (Chicago)
9. High school females place either one or both hands on their hips when they are putting males "on the spot." (A-11) (Chicago)	7. High school students are more comfortable with visual images than with sound images. (A-11) (Chicago)	12. Good readers mumble words intentionally. (D-6-5) (Chicago)	11. High school students seem confused about whether they should hate all whites or just some whites. (D-10-1) (Chicago)	11. The poorer readers are the first to volunteer for reading dramatic parts. (D-6-5) (Chicago)
10. Disagreement often results in a high school female striking a high school male. (A-11) (Chicago)			12. High school male students feel the need to have the best of anything under discussion. (A-11) (Chicago)	12. Reading comprehension is significantly better among high school students when dramatic reading is engaged in. (A-11) (Chicago)
11. When singled out by a female teacher for discipline, high school students glare at her, their eyes very wide and fixed. (A-11) (Chicago)			13. There is in high school male students a negative reaction toward active black females. (A-11) (Chicago)	
12. High school students move very close to whomever they are talk-			14. High school students think it is acceptable for women to have illegitimate children.	

PHASE TWO ETHNIC PROFILE: BLACK AMERICAN (HIGH SCHOOL STUDENTS CHICAGO)

Nonverbal Communication	Orientation Modes	Verbal Communication	Social Value Patterns	Intellectual Modes
ing to as if they had something very confidential to say. (D-8-3) (Chicago) 13. High school male students have a very suave attitude toward female teachers and engage in a lot of smooth bantering aimed at the teacher. (A-11) (Chicago) 14. High school male students slump a lot in their seats. (D-5-6) (Chicago) 15. High school male students tend to walk with their heads tilted to one side. (D-4-7) (Chicago) 16. High school students, especially males,		(D-5-6) (Chicago) 13. "Pimp walk" is a gait that combines a bouncy step with shuffling. Young males often walk this way. (A-11) (Chicago) 14. References to mother in discussion between male high school students is frequent; these references tend to become insults and sometimes result in physical fighting. (A-11) (Chicago) 15. In group discussion situations, there does not appear to be an orderly exchange of ideas. (D-9-2) (Chicago) 16. Male high school students flaunt the use of curse words. (D-5-6)	(D-5-6) (Chicago) 15. High school students do not justify their present behaviors with future goals. (A-11) (Chicago) 16. Parents of high school students exhibit concern about their children's progress. (D-10-1) (Chicago) 17. Mothers are predominantly the ones having contact with the school. (A-11) (Chicago) 18. Many mothers worked. (A-11) (Chicago) 19. Older daughters often replaced the mother in school contacts. (A-11) (Chicago) 20. Older children have the responsibility of	

PHASE TWO ETHNIC PROFILE: BLACK AMERICAN (HIGH SCHOOL STUDENTS CHICAGO)

Nonverbal Communication	Orientation Modes	Verbal Communication	Social Value Patterns	Intellectual Modes
loiter around outside the classroom. (A-11) (Chicago) 17. High school students wear berets and pom-pom hats to class (D-4-7) (Chicago) 18. While standing in a group, there is a lot of shifting of the body position so that the physical formation of the group is always changing. (A-11) (Chicago) 19. Many of the interactions between male and female students were physical with touching and pretend sparring characteristics. (D-10-1) (Chicago)		(Chicago) 17. High school students use onomatopoeia sound effects very freely. (A-11) (Chicago) 18. High school students do not recognize their speech patterns when these are pointed out to them. (D-5-6) (Chicago) 19. Poorer readers are usually the ones that verbalize the most in class. (D-6-5) (Chicago) 20. Poorer readers are the first to volunteer for reading dramatic parts. (D-6-5) (Chicago) 21. The term, "bummy," is very popular; it means "nasty." (A-11) (Chicago)	bringing younger children to and from school. (A-11) (Chicago) 21. High school male students aspired not to fear the consequences of their actions. (A-11) (Chicago) 22. High school male students aspired to achieve great sexual prowess. (A-11) (Chicago)	

significant proportion of the group in question. We also needed to evaluate the success of the actions we would take as well as the continued viability of our generalizations.

To begin with, we recognized that our collection of inputs indicated the need for continued observations. For instance, there was an apparent contradiction between the entries under intellectual modes, which noted that the words to many songs are remembered, that new learning entails a great deal of vocalization, and that oral spelling seems to be more readily accomplished than written spelling, and the entry under orientation modes that noted a higher visual than sound orientation.

It might be that the apparent contradiction involved differences in the nature of student participation required by the teacher, that is, whether the teacher involved the students passively or actively. Black students might be more efficient orally when asked to perform actively in front of the class, but when listening, without the requirement of active performance, they might prefer visual stimuli. Obviously, before any instructional steps could be taken in this instance, some directed observations of visual and oral behavior in the learning process would need to be undertaken. There were some specific questions that observations might answer. For instance, when students are passively involved in school learning, as occurs during a lecture, what are the approaches to learning for which they demonstrate preference? Do they want the lecture in some kind of outline form? Do they summarize the lecture aloud in their own words while the lecture is going on? at the end of the lecture?

Under the aspect of verbal communication, there is the generalization that black high school students do not appear to engage in orderly exchanges of ideas during discussion. Since it is questionable that any group of human beings would persist in exchanging ideas in a way that would impede *their* understanding of the ideas being discussed, it is likely that the system used by the observees for exchanging ideas is different from the ones used by the observers. What needs to be understood more fully is the system or discussion mode(s) used by the observees;

thus observations of discussion modes should be given special attention.

Under social value patterns there is an entry noting that high school students do not justify their present behaviors with future goals. I suppose (though I really do not know) that this entry was prompted by the student teachers trying to convince high school students that they ought to study some topic or other, even if it did not interest them, because it would be useful to them in the future. There are numerous questions that need to be explored in this regard. For instance, are some future-oriented concerns taken more seriously than others, and, if so, what are they? How do youngsters think of their own futures? With hope and expectation? With indifference? Exactly how do black high school students justify what they do in school? The money motive would seem to be relevant to this question, judging from one or two of the other entries.

Some of the generalizations, of course, did not seem to lead clearly toward any specific kinds of instructional methodology. Others, such as those indicating a preference among black males for individually oriented, somewhat theatrical performance with the class acting as audience, had direct implications for instructional methodologies. What we finally did was reorder the format of the generalizations into worksheets, which allowed us to note the kinds of activities and/or inquiries that we would try to undertake in response to specific generalizations. The entries were still organized according to aspects, but each aspect was listed on separate sheets so that there would be space to hypothesize and/or inquire about generalizations. A few samples follow.

Nonverbal Communication	*Possible Activities and/or Inquiries to be Undertaken*
1. High school males often walk with a proud gait that	–Need to ascertain the meaning(s) of this walk: when used, for what purposes. Should a teacher be offended when this walk is used by a young high school male?

Nonverbal Communication	*Possible Activities and/or Inquiries to be Undertaken*
combines a bouncy step with shuffling and is called the "pimp walk." (A-11) (Chicago)	
2. To indicate agreement, two high school males often slap their palms together, using one or both hands, and then take a step backwards away from each other. (A-11) (Chicago)	–No direct relevance for teaching.
3. To greet each other, high school males would slap their palms together, using one or both hands, and then take a step backwards away from each other. (A-11) (Chicago)	–No direct relevance for teaching.
4. When the teacher approached high school students, they	–Need to ascertain teacher's own reaction to backing away behavior of youngster. –Need to ascertain the meaning(s) expressed by the youngsters backing away.

Nonverbal Communication	*Possible Activities and/or Inquiries to be Undertaken*
back away. (A-11) (Chicago)	
5. High school males rarely stand straight; they usually lean. (A-11) (Chicago)	–Consideration of tendency many teachers have to tell students to "stand up straight." Would this be unduly offensive?
6. High school students who do not do well in school prefer to sit at the very back of the room. (A-11) (Chicago)	–Would redirecting teacher's positions when teaching toward the back of the room help these students to pay closer attention? –Is there a tendency for the teacher to ignore the very back of the room when asking questions?
7. High school males touch females, often holding them by the forearm, in order to get their attention. (A-11) (Chicago)	–Need to ascertain how this kind of touching is interpreted by the teacher. Are meanings other than "attention" attached to this kind of touching?
8. High school females place either one or both hands on their hips when they are angry. (A-11) (Chicago)	–If this behavior is directed toward a teacher, should it be interpreted as insulting? Should it be confronted openly or ignored?
9. High school females place either one or	–If this happens during a class discussion, it might be helpful to divert attention away from the female, either directing attention toward an object in question or

Nonverbal Communication	*Possible Activities and/or Inquiries to be Undertaken*
both hands on their hips when they are putting males "on the spot." (A-11) (Chicago)	toward some topic not related to male-female interaction. This might avoid embarrassment for the young male.
10. Disagreement often results in a high school female striking a high school male. (A-11) (Chicago)	–Does this occur during regular class lessons? –Is this a serious blow or just playful? How is it interpreted by the high school male? –Is this likely to lead to a serious incident or repeated periods of disruptive behavior?
11. When singled out by a female teacher for discipline, high school students glare at her, their eyes very wide and fixed. (A-11) (Chicago)	–Is there any link between this behavior and violence in the classroom? –Is this kind of behavior best dealt with by "facing down" or confronting the student with a similar behavior? –Need to ascertain whether this is a sign that the student can no longer cope with the discussion in words. Should calm discussion be encouraged at this point or delayed?
12. High school students move very close to whomever they are talking to as if they had something very confidential to say. (D-8-3) (Chicago)	–Need to ascertain how this "close" distance is interpreted by the teacher. What are the meanings intended? Do these correspond with teacher's interpretation? Should the teacher try to increase the spatial distance with students?
13. High school male students have a very	–How should bantering be interpreted? Is there a point or particular set of topics that would make the bantering unacceptable to members of the same ethnic

Nonverbal Communication	*Possible Activities and/or Inquiries to be Undertaken*
suave attitude toward female teachers and engage in a lot of smooth bantering aimed at the teacher. (A-11) (Chicago)	group? –Should the teacher try to stop this bantering? –Should the teacher engage in the bantering?
14. High school male students slump a lot in their seats. (D-5-6) (Chicago)	–Need to ascertain how this "slump" affects the teacher's own reactions. Consideration of tendency many teachers have to tell students to "sit up in their seats." Is this unduly offensive? –Need to ascertain whether "slump" interferes with classroom attentiveness during learning situations, i.e., does slump indicate inattentiveness, boredom, sleepiness?

Verbal Communication	*Possible Activities and/or Inquiries to be Undertaken*
1. The use of "mama" is preferred to "mother." (A-11) (Chicago)	–No direct relevance for teaching. –There might be some usefulness in exploring how youngsters react to these two terms under stressful circumstances as, for example, when being told they will need to bring their mother or father to school to avoid suspension.
2. High school students have difficulty reading aloud literature that has dialogues in black dialect. (A-11) (Chicago)	–Care needs to be taken not to expect black youngsters to read black dialect anymore competently than white youngsters. Black dialect may *not* be the native language of the black students in the class. Difficulty in reading aloud may even occur among native speakers if they have little or no occasion to read their dialect aloud. –Possibly both whites and blacks could be asked to read black dialect aloud. Some caution may be necessary with this activity for it could lead to some competition between blacks and whites. Literature containing other English dialects might also be used so that no one group would have the edge. Some grammatical

Verbal Communication	*Possible Activities and/or Inquiries to be Undertaken*
	comparisons of the dialects read aloud could also be undertaken.
3. In an argument, high school male students go out of their way to have the last word over the female. (A-11) (Chicago)	–Does this apply to female teachers? –Is having the last word with females associated with some deeply held social value patterns? What are these? –If a female teacher needs to reprimand a black male student, would a private conference after school be better than a discussion during class? (Possible pro's and con's?)
4. There was a lot of very audible laughing in the group conversation of high school students. (A-11) (Chicago)	–No direct relevance to teaching other than an exploration of the teacher's own reactions to such laughter and some effort to verify the validity of the teacher's interpretations.
5. High school students dislike having their own names mispro-nounced. (A-11) (Chicago)	–Special attention needs to be given to learning the full names and correct pronounciation of students' names.
6. High school students only approximate the pronounciation of a teacher's name. (A-11) (Chicago)	–Given generalization #5, it is necessary to ascertain whether there is disrespect when students regularly mispronounce the teacher's name. It might be helpful to classroom management to emphasize the correct pronounciation of all names including that of the teacher.

Verbal Communication	*Possible Activities and/or Inquiries to be Undertaken*
7. Everything high school students say is loud. (D-4-7) (Chicago)	−"Loudness" needs to be investigated more thoroughly. Do students and the teacher have the same understanding of what is "loud"? Are there certain situations when "loud" talk goes on? Is it present even when students are productively involved in class activities? Is it a sign of boredom?
8. High school students refuse to repeat anything once they have said it. (A-11) (Chicago)	−Is this true under all circumstances? If not, what kinds of circumstances can be associated with the refusal to repeat?
9. High school students do not say "please" and "thank you." (D-10-1) (Chicago)	−Ascertain if this is *always* true. −Need to determine why "please" and "thank you" are avoided. Possibly there might be other terms that could be substituted and serve the same purpose, but avoid some of the resistance associated with these.

Intellectual Patterns	*Possible Activities and/or Inquiries to be Undertaken*
1. High school students are not mechanically competent. (D-6-5) (Chicago)	−Need to ascertain whether mechanical competence increases with some kinds of machinery, i.e., is familiarity a factor? −Need to determine the influence upon school performance (e.g., do hand calculators pose unexpected difficulties?).
2. Thinking in abstractions is difficult for high school students. (A-11) (Chicago)	−Need to ascertain in which areas or with what topics abstractions seem to be handled more easily. Possibly a particular concept can be taught to different classes using different topics as the teaching vehicle (e.g., the concept of free enterprise via such topics as starting a small business, the trading of professional basketball /football/baseball players, or farming as a free enterprise business).

Intellectual Patterns	*Possible Activities and/or Inquiries to be Undertaken*
3. High school students remember the complete words to a surprising number of popular songs. (A-11) (Chicago)	–Use words of songs and singing to teach important events of history such as Civil War and the carpet baggers. –Use songs to explore changing social perspectives about slavery, women's roles, travel, and the like. –Use songs to exemplify different poetic forms. –Compare words of songs from different cultural groups.
4. In learning something new, high school students vocalize a great deal. (A-11) (Chicago)	–Need to understand contradiction between this entry and the one indicating visual perference. –Plan periods of small group interaction for new learning. Groups should be so organized that each student can talk about what is being learned.
5. High school students are desirous of performing. (A-11) (Chicago)	–Arrange classroom situations so that as many students as possible can perform individually while the class acts as audience. –Need to ascertain which types of performance attract interest of students, i.e., singing, reciting, role playing, and the like.
6. There seems to be little correlation in high school students between the amount of homework accomplished at home and classroom learning. (D-7-4) (Chicago)	–Need to ascertain type of homework assigned and whether there is a clear relationship to class work. –Need to ascertain whether students not doing homework are those who do best in school. Assignments and classwork may be too easy and lacking in challenge.
7. High school students are	–Arrange learning situations for writing such that students can dictate what they want to say, the teacher

Intellectual Patterns	*Possible Activities and/or Inquiries to be Undertaken*
frequently able to spell words orally but not in writing. (D-5-6) (Chicago)	(or a student) writes it on the board, and other students copy each sentence as it is written. A variation of this would allow each student to add a sentence to the composition in round robin fashion.
8. When high school students reach a certain point of frustration in learning something, they do not work harder or more to "get" it. (D-9-2) (Chicago)	–Ascertain specific nonverbal clues indicating a "certain point of frustration." –Allow student to stop participating; develop a special activity to help student understand and assign this activity *privately* to student at next class meeting.

Social Value Patterns	*Possible Activities and/or Inquiries to be Undertaken*
1. High school students have an active dislike of being categorized. (A-11) (Chicago)	–Avoid using generalizations as comments about a student when giving instructions or reprimanding. For example, the teacher says, "Blacks are good jazz musicians," and then turns to a student who is black and asks him or her to do a report on jazz. Or the teacher says, "You're a real performer. Take the part of Hamlet."
2. It is usual for high school students to say they would do anything for money, but their actions do not bear out this verbalization. (A-11) (Chicago)	–Exploring wealth in the sense of "what money means to me" might make a social studies or English topic that would spark the interest of students not usually interested in these subjects. –Need to ascertain what goals are ethnically more important than becoming rich. This might clarify when future goals can be used as incentives for school study.

Social Value Patterns	*Possible Activities and/or Inquiries to be Undertaken*
3. There is a strong tendency for high school students to help each other in class. (A-11) (Chicago)	–Provision for students to help each other needs to be incorporated in lesson plans frequently.
4. A motto of high school students seems to be: "Do whatever you can get away with." (A-11) (Chicago)	–Need to ascertain the types of beliefs underlying this behavior. Is the institution actively blamed for perceived injustices? Is this the motto among personal friends? –The motto itself might be used as a topic in values clarification teaching for a civics class.
5. Horoscopes are very popular among high school students. (A-11) (Chicago)	–Could be related in a variety of ways to science studies. For example, the basic assumptions of astrology could be compared with those of astronomy or physics or sciences in general.
6. It is desirable, though often not possible, for high school male students to wear expensive, flashy clothes. (A-11) (Chicago)	–Need to ascertain the social significance of flashy clothes and whether some activities intended to "show off" clothes can be negatively interpreted by some teachers or so interfered with by some teachers as to create extremely high resentment in the student.
7. While high school students seem to be very militant in	–Need to ascertain whether this is an ethnic avoidance of conflict/confrontation or simply lack of interest in topics or types of discussions employed in the classroom.

Social Value Patterns	Possible Activities and/or Inquiries to be Undertaken
conversation, they take few positions against anything. (A-11) (Chicago)	–Need to ascertain the precise characteristics of militancy, including the subjects that seem to excite such behavior. –Need to ascertain what behaviors give teachers an impression of militancy and accuracy of impressions.
8. Many high school males express the desire to become "pimps." (D-9-2) (Chicago)	–Because of multi-ethnic values present in schools, this topic cannot be explored directly with students, but might be viewed from the perspective of studying the personal importance of money, suggested above as a topic of special interest to be used for social studies or English.

The foregoing list of activities and inquiries formed a kind of loose plan of action, which teachers could undertake while they returned to data collecting for more phase one material. In subsequent generalizing stages of phase two, teachers could discuss the results of the activities and inquiries that each had tried on her or his own. Thus, phase two could be not only a period of revising tentative generalizations regarding a group's ethnic behavior, but one of determining possible instructional improvements, areas of further study, and assessment of activities undertaken to meet specific ethnic traits.

SELF-ORIENTED TEACHER PROFILE

What became progressively more disturbing as I engaged in these phase two sessions was that my students, as teachers and observers of ethnicity, tended to emphasize inquiries and activities that concerned the behaviors of the group being studied, while planning little to explore the influences of their own behaviors. When I began teaching a class in ethnic diversities at

The University of Michigan-Flint, I tried to counteract this tendency by employing another modification of the ethnic profile format. The five aspects were related to specific activities such as "giving an important explanation" and "a student chewing gum in class." Since most of my students were teaching in the schools, they could observe the behavior of their classes or, at least, become more aware of their own behaviors during each of the specific activities. After a period of this kind of self-observation, they met in groups of four in a phase two effort to generalize about their own behaviors. A brief sample of these efforts follows.

If these self-oriented teacher profiles were pursued sufficiently, they might lead to an effective exploration of the nature of scholastic ethnicity. The tentative generalizations included in the preceding sample are indicative of a number of further observations that could be profitably undertaken. The various references to increased and decreased voice volume are likely to be accompanied by other vocal traits that may carry considerable meaning and/or different meaning for students of different ethnic backgrounds. Exactly what kinds of behaviors are permissible when everyone must look like he or she is paying attention? What conflicts are perceived between friendliness and keeping discipline? Can a persistent difference in patterns of behavior be related to different times of the school day and at different points in a class hour?

The ethnic backgrounds of teachers' own heritages would need to be described and compared with those of other teachers as well as with scholastic ethnicity. The origins of many different kinds of tensions could thus become the object of open, somewhat objective discussion.

It is my belief that the very processes involved in using the ethnic profile in its various modes sensitizes teachers to multi-ethnic diversity and improves their capacity to teach effectively in a multi-ethnic situation. Though I am aware that my students have difficulty maintaining an acceptable level of objectivity in the development of entries, I am convinced that the effort to achieve such inputs and the experience of talking these over

SELF-ORIENTED TEACHER PROFILE (SOUTHERN MICHIGAN, ELEMENTARY TEACHERS)

Specific Activity	Nonverbal Communication	Verbal Communication	Orientation Modes	Social Value Patterns	Intellectual Modes
Giving an important explanation	Stand erect in center of front of room. (A-4) Avoid smiling. (A-4) Furrowing the brow. (D-1-3) Arms bent at elbows with hand movements held with a rectangle roughly approximating upper torso. (D-3-1)	Voice volume louder than usual. (A-4) Tendency to use formal grammatical structure. (A-4) Minimal humor used. (A-4)	Nice spring weather seen through classroom windows makes it difficult to give a serious explanation. (A-4)	Everyone must seem to be paying attention during an important explanation. Those who give any other impression, even though not disruptive, register negatively on the teacher's opinion. (D-3-1)	Questions asked before the point of an explanation is reached are annoying. (A-4) When questions are invited, none are asked even though later on it becomes clear that students do have questions. (D-3-1)
Trying to attract class attention	Stand erect in center of front of room. (A-4) Tilt head slightly upward with lips slightly parted as if ready to speak. (A-4)	Begin to write on board without an introduction. (A-4) Take on vocal characteristics of making an announcement.	Require students to "fix up" or put the room in order to develop an atmosphere conducive to paying attention. (D-2-2)	It is offensive to the teacher when various efforts at attracting attention are ignored. Students seem disrespectful. (D-2-2)	Use references to the coming test as a way of capturing attention. (D-3-1)

Specific Activity	Nonverbal Communication	Verbal Communication	Orientation Modes	Social Value Patterns	Intellectual Modes
Trying to attract class attention	Raise hand, palm toward class. (D-2-2) Clear throat. (A-4) Slam a book down on desk. (D-2-2)	(A-4) Increase voice volume. (A-4)			
Regaining the attention of one or two students	Stop talking and stare at student(s). (A-4) Walk toward student(s) until unusually close. (D-3-1)	Increase voice volume. (A-4) Mention individual student's name. (A-4) Add a personal comment about student not paying attention as part of the explanation. (D-2-2)		Sometimes refer to the disturbance as being rude, especially because of interfering with the rights of other students in the class. (A-4) Test is used as a threat. (D-3-1)	Use references to the coming test as a way of capturing attention. (D-3-1)
Student chewing gum in class	Widen eyes and stare at offending student. (A-4) Narrow eyes and stare at offending	Reference to rules made in a very low voice without mentioning student's name.	Time of day seems to influence degree of reaction. (D-2-2) Morning increases	Noticeable gum-chewing impairs student's image for teacher. (A-4) There is a sense of	

Specific Activity	Nonverbal Communication	Verbal Communication	Orientation Modes	Social Value Patterns	Intellectual Modes
Student chewing gum in class	student. (D-3-1) With small smile on face, point to wastebasket. (A-4)	(A-4) Direct reprimand (A-4) *but* no agreement on how reprimand is carried out.	reaction. (D-2-2) Afternoon increases reaction. (D-2-2)	disrespect for the teacher when gum chewing is very noticeable. (D-3-1)	
Trying to be friendly with the class as a whole	Body relaxed, with arms folded, weight more on one leg. (A-4) Upper torso held slightly toward the class. (A-4) Lips held in a slight smile with frequent full smiles. (A-4)	Use voice as though talking with a small group of friends. (A-4) Sometimes joke with a group of students, using increased volume of voice. (D-3-1)	Friendliness with class as a whole usually occurs in late afternoon. (A-4) Friendliness with class as a whole usually occurs toward the end of a lesson. (A-4)	The teacher being friendly may undermine the teacher's ability to keep discipline. (D-2-2)	Friendliness improves conditions for student learning. (A-4)

with others, as well as planning strategies for inquiry and improvement, are of immense benefit to them as teachers; I have had many testimonials to this effect. The enterprise is exciting, but it admittedly needs far more individual involvement of teachers before its qualities can be truly known.

TEACHING IN THE MULTI-ETHNIC CLASSROOM

Up to this point, the development of ethnic profiles has been presented as a way of sensitizing the interpersonal behavior of teachers and the instructional methodologies they adopt to the pluralistic circumstances of America's public schools. The ethnic profile may also be viewed as a direct source of both instructional methodologies and of classroom materials for ethnic studies. For example, in the discussion of verbal communication (Chapter IV), it was pointed out that teachers might begin to develop some tentative rules about a neighborhood dialect by organizing the way they listen to youngsters talk. Even if this is done for only a few major grammatical features, it holds promise of increasing teachers' understanding of the structural difficulties children might encounter in learning the grammar of standard English. If, on the other hand, teachers were to ask their students to investigate their own (and perhaps their friends') dialect, a powerful instructional methodology for teaching grammatical processes and an inquiry into these might be achieved.

To introduce the idea to students, teachers might initially have to do some structured listening on their own and concentrate on one or two linguistic features. Suppose half the class is composed of black Americans from the same neighborhood, a fourth is of Chicano origin, and the remaining students, all white, of blue-collar background. They will need to listen for a similar feature in three different native tongues.

Listening to black American students, they may find that a number of them do not use the *'s* present in the standard English possessive. They may hear phrases such as *John cousin* and *boy ball*. Such phrases are probably indicative of a language rule in the students' native tongue. If, after a concentrated effort at listening to the way black American students express the possessive, they still hear the *'s* omitted with regularity, they are then justified in making a hypothesis about the possessive that they can share with students. The hypothesis might be that in the black dialect spoken by members of the class the way nouns are placed in relation to each other expresses ownership. For instance, *boy father* indicates that the father belongs to the boy, while *father boy* indicates that the boy belongs to the father. It is really not so important that teachers be absolutely correct in their hypotheses but that they can give examples of students' language back to them to examine the structure of their own speech and to compare with the rules of standard English.

Listening to Mexican-American students, teachers may find that the *'s* is also infrequently used. Instead, they hear expressions such as *the dog of John* and *the lessons of the little girl* repeatedly. While the use of *of* to express possession in standard English is correct, it is not the most usual form. Teachers who note this observation repeatedly verified in the speech of Mexican-American students might reasonably hypothesize that the possessive in their native tongue is expressed by placing *of* between the noun that is the owner and the noun that is possessed.

The two above hypotheses make it possible for teachers to present two grammatical models of the possessive to students besides the standard English *'s* version. The following diagram of the three models indicates how inquiry into comparative grammatical structure can be introduced to a class of multiethnic background.

Students could be asked, say as a homework assignment, to listen to their friends and neighbors at home and to decide whether the teacher's model of the possessive is correct. Each student's expertise in his or her own native tongue should be emphasized. Each could be asked to look for exceptions to the rule. Students might also be asked to explain in their own words the grammatical differences between the dialects, and, finally, following the rules, they might convert sentences of their own from one dialect to another. Of course, if real competency were

Comparison of the Possessive

Black American	Noun (possessor)	+	Noun (possessed by possessor)
Chicano:	Noun (possessed by the possessor)	+ of {indicates that preceding noun is possessor}	+ (article)Noun (possessor)
Standard English	Noun (possessor)	+ 's added to noun to make possessor	+ Noun (possessed by possessor)
Less frequent standard English	Noun (possessed by the possessor)	+ of {indicates that preceding noun is possessor}	+ (article)Noun (possessor)

achieved, entire short stories could be converted.

To involve youngsters more fully and actively in the process of identifying grammatical rules, they could develop a checklist to guide their listening. Such a checklist might include the grammatical features to be investigated, their linguistic forms or grammatical rules with examples, and the approximate frequency with which these have been heard.

The aspect of social value patterns might also be an important source of instructional materials, especially in any analysis of the ideals and goals for living that Americans hold in common and the differences that may exist about such ideals and goals from one ethnic group to another. To ascertain what might be considered nationally held goals, advertisements in widely circulated magazines could be analyzed as they represent, to some extent, what is considered desirable in American life. Advertisers are not experts in the sense that sociologists and anthropologists may be, but a successful advertiser must have some sensitivity about what will appeal to people and /or create a sense of identity with products or services.

The repeated appearance of certain kinds of images, activities, environments, and the like over the course of several

SAMPLE OF A GRAMMATICAL CHECKLIST

Grammatical Feature	Examples	Frequency observed per one day							
		5	10	15	20	25	30	35	40
1. Formation of Plural a. Regular standard English addition of -s.	1a.								
b. Omission of -s.	1b.								
c. Divergent addition of -s.	1c.								
d. Other modes for conveying plural.	1d.								
2. Formation of Possessive a. Regular standard English addition of -'s.	2a.								
b. Omission of -'s.	2b.								
c. Nonstandard addition of -'s.	2c.								
d. Other modes for conveying possessive.	2d.								
3. Formation of Simple Present a. Regular standard English formation i.e., addition of -s on third person singular and no addition in all other persons.	3a.								
b. Omission of -s in third person singular.	3b.								
c. Addition of -s in other persons.	3c.								
d. Other modes for forming simple present.	3d.								

years is indicative that advertisers have met with some success using them, that is, they hit a responding chord in Americans. An analysis of advertisements could be undertaken by students during which full-page advertisements are collected from magazines over a three-month period. Students could share the advertisements, and a set of simple questions could be used to guide the analysis of *each* advertisement. For instance:

1. What do the people look like? (hair coloring, complexion, sex, build, demeanor, i.e., smiling, serious, frazzled)
2. What are they doing? (skiing, cleaning, etc.)
3. What is the setting like? (expensive house, outdoors, etc.)
4. What does the advertisement seem to be saying about the people and their way of life? Give your impressions.

In small groups, students could try to summarize those responses that appear frequently. Obviously, this will be easier for the physical descriptions of people than for what the advertisements say about people and their way of life. In any case, students should at least make the effort to summarize.

Up to this point the activity will involve the entire class without ethnic distinctions, but at this juncture the teacher could point out that, while we all share many of the ideals and desires noted in the study of advertisements, there are characteristics and goals that each of us has because we are unique individuals, and because we are members of a group that has raised us, loved us, and left us with a heritage that we will pass on to our children. The first assignment might be to explore one's own personal ideals of what a good way to live might be in, say, a brief composition, which need not be shared with anyone. The second step might be to organize small groups who willingly identify with an ethnic group and have them, as ethnic groups, discuss what they believe is desirable, important, and possible in their own futures. What do magazine ads say to them regarding their ideals? Students who do not identify ethnically with others in the class could be asked to think about how advertisements might be different in the future and why? What changes in our values will underlie such differences?

Similar analyses could be undertaken using newspaper comic strips. For example, comic strips limited to family-type subjects and appearing during a given period of time might be described by students after answering a set of questions, which the students, themselves, could devise (e.g., How often do parents discuss money and family budget? How often are children scolded? Who does the scolding?) Again, the class summary of observations could serve as a way of exploring one's own family life and the family life of one's ethnic group.

All the aspects of ethnicity hold implications for how classroom teaching might be organized. If a teacher realizes that different kinds of discussion modes are used by several ethnic groups in a classroom, lesson plans can be designed so that one and then another discussion mode is incorporated. For example, day one of a unit might be intended to generate enthusiasm. A topic likely to excite discussion might be used and students would be allowed to discuss it in as free a fashion as possible. Several minutes before the end of the class, the teacher could summarize on the board whatever points seem to have come from the discussion. Day two would feature a one-at-a-time discussion to make sure each student understood the preceding day's discussion. Day three could be planned for small group discussion, day four might be a lecture, and day five might be another day open to whatever discussion modes arise.

Nothing is new in what has just been described, except the conscious intent to make provisions *within the lesson plan* for ethnic diversity. Recognizing differences in the qualities of attention span or in the diverse ways ethnic groups prefer to exercise their intellectual abilities becomes meaningful in public education when teachers make a conscious effort to incorporate these insights into either instructional methodology or the curriculum. The ethnic profiles I have proposed are a contribution to what I hope can become a truly pluralistic orientation to public education.

Epilogue-Prologue

A work like this doesn't come to an end. . . . There is so much left to be done or done better; still I feel good that I have at least started.

I have great hopes for the possibilities and the breadth of the ethnic profiles. I envision a host of action researchers developing for themselves and for others an interethnic sensitivity and deeper understanding.

All the aspects of ethnicity need other researchers to improve their conception and achieve a better quality of data. In a sense, all that I have written is a call for the help of others. This is an invitation to a new way of perceiving research and a new way of joining efforts so that the ethnic differences of being human may be better understood and better loved.

Developing an Instrument for Describing Nonverbal Communication

Some excellent work has been done recently in exploring nonverbal communication systems by use of portable television and slow motion pictures. This author had the good fortune of participating in a one-day seminar led by the practicing anthropologist Fred Erickson, now of Harvard. He spent several hours demonstrating how repetition and slowing down nonverbal interactions, which are possible with the slow motion camera, could aid in analyzing body movement synchronization and subliminal comprehension or noncomprehension between two conversing people. The observations achieved by Erickson were clearly far more objective and capable of intersubjectivity than any that could be made by the average teacher in a classroom. However, because of the prohibitive expense and complexity of the visual aids involved, my inventory and checklist forms, adapted to the circumstances of the average teacher, seem a more attractive mode for action researching.

If nonverbal descriptions of sufficient breadth and consistency of form are to be achieved by action researching, then some

instrument suited to the classroom needs to be developed; I
have taken a few initial steps in that direction.

The first major problem I faced in developing a nonverbal
observation checklist was establishing some sort of classification system of classroom situations. The situation or context
within which a student behaves in certain nonverbal ways aids
in clarifying the meanings people connect with those behaviors.
It also serves as a basis for comparing nonverbal observations
made by different observers in different schools.

For the purposes intended, the categories of classroom talk
developed for the Flanders System of Interaction Analysis[1]
seem well suited. These categories are believed to cover the
range of verbal interactions that occur during the average
classroom lesson. As reference points for observing nonverbal
interaction, they not only offer a complete analysis of the kinds
of verbal behaviors found in the classroom but a consistent
mode of describing under what general conditions an observation is to be made.

Flanders' ten categories offer ten classroom situations during
which the nonverbal or diakinesic systems of students and
teachers may be described. The categories and related definitions for the Flanders System of Interaction Analysis follow:

TEACHER TALK		1. ACCEPTS FEELING: Accepts and clari-fies the feeling tone of the students in a non-threatening manner. Feelings may be positive or negative. Predicting or recall-ing feelings are included.
		2. PRAISES OR ENCOURAGES: Praises or encourages student action or behavior. Jokes that release tension, not at the ex-pense of another individual, nodding head or saying, "um hm?" or "go on" are in-cluded.
	INDIRECT INFLUENCE	3. ACCEPTS OR USES IDEAS OF STU-DENT: Clarifying, building, or develop-ing ideas suggested by a student. As a teacher brings more of his own ideas into play, shift to category five.

TEACHER TALK	**INDIRECT INFLUENCE**	4. ASKS QUESTIONS: Asking a question about content or procedure with the intent that a student answer.
	DIRECT INFLUENCE	5. LECTURING: Giving facts or opinions about content or procedure; expressing his own ideas, asking rhetorical questions. 6. GIVING DIRECTIONS: Directions, commands, or orders to which a student is expected to comply. 7. CRITICIZING OR JUSTIFYING AUTHORITY: Statements intended to change student behavior from nonacceptable to acceptable pattern; bawling someone out; stating why the teacher is doing what he is doing; extreme self-reference.
STUDENT TALK		8. STUDENT TALK—RESPONSE: A student makes a predictable response to teacher. Teacher initiates the contact or solicits student statement and sets limits to what the student says. 9. STUDENT TALK—INITIATION: Talk by students which they initiate. Unpredictable statements in response to teacher. Shift from 8 to 9 as student introduces own ideas. 10. SILENCE OR CONFUSION: Pauses, short periods of silence, and periods of confusion in which communication cannot be understood by the observer.

The next problem I faced was developing some means for describing nonverbal behavior so that the descriptions could be referred to across time and place in an intersubjective fashion. Birdwhistell[2] has already developed a notational system for analyzing body motion and gesture. While really a simple graphic language, it contains too many diverse symbols for the average teacher to gain command of its use.

Birdwhistell's symbols are designed to include eight body sections. Each body section has a series of base symbols (e.g., total head: H hh, face:oö△, shoulder, arm and wrist: #< >.)[3] These symbols are then further explicated by symbols describing the motions made by each section of the body (e.g., single raised brow,–∧, eyes upward,‌ꙩꙩ).[4] It occurred to me that this glossary of symbols could be simplified if the eight sections of the body were listed on a single form along with the more important subsections of the body. Motions could then be expressed by generalized symbols applicable to any part of the body. While this method probably makes the resulting descriptions too gross for micro-analysis of body movements and gestures, it does permit the quick recording of macro-observations of body movement.

Some examples to clarify the kind of system I developed might be useful. Birdwhistell suggests a specialized symbol to indicate rolled eyes: ♂♂.[5] In the glossary suggested, the symbol for roll and rolling↻ , would be placed in the space for eye descriptions and indicate rolling or rolled eyes. The direction of the rolling motion is indicated by the arrow.ꙩꙩ. Closed eyes are represented in Birdwhistell's glossary with the symbol∏Ʋ∏[6] In my modified glossary, the general movement symbol for closed or closing, [ ], would be placed in the appropriate space on the sheet. Similarly, wide or flaring nostrils, which, in essence, is opening the nostril passages to wider than usual proportions, would be described in my modified glossary by placing the general movement symbol for open or opening,] [, alongisde the row indicating nose. There is no space on the sheet for nostrils since the kind of movement attributed to the nose would, in most instances, indicate the part of the nose involved.

There are, of course, some movements that are unique to certain parts of the body. For example, the tongue used to moisten the lips is unique to the mouth. In such a case, an observer would use abbreviated forms of standard English, placed in the appropriate space on the form (e.g., "lip wipe" might be used). The glossary includes a list of such abbreviated standard English descriptions, but observers will often have to coin their own. It is felt that abbreviated descriptions combined with generalized movement symbols and a single-sheet form listing the various parts of the body could adequately describe body movements.

The glossary, still in its developmental stages, is given below:

GLOSSARY FOR NONVERBAL OBSERVATION CHECKLIST

Basic Movement Symbols

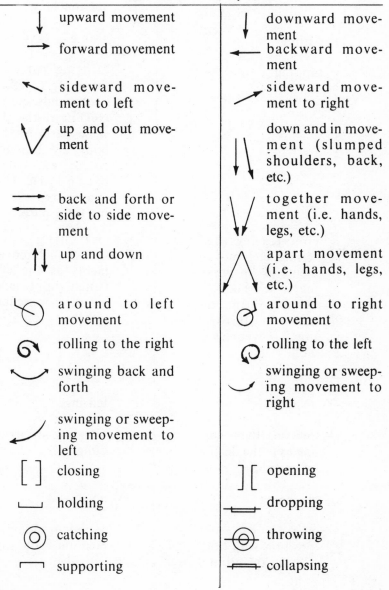

↓	upward movement	↓	downward movement
→	forward movement	←	backward movement
↖	sideward movement to left	↗	sideward movement to right
V	up and out movement	↓↓	down and in movement (slumped shoulders, back, etc.)
	back and forth or side to side movement	V	together movement (i.e. hands, legs, etc.)
↑↓	up and down	Λ	apart movement (i.e. hands, legs, etc.)
	around to left movement		around to right movement
	rolling to the right		rolling to the left
	swinging back and forth		swinging or sweeping movement to right
	swinging or sweeping movement to left		
[ ]	closing	] [	opening
	holding		dropping
⊚	catching		throwing
	supporting		collapsing

Basic Movement Symbols

⊢—	pushing	—⊣	pulling
⊢—⊣	extending, stretching	⋏	bending, folding
I	touching	⊥̄	not touching
⊥	patting	⊥⊥	hitting
I I	tapping or drumming		

bringing parts of the body together (feet, hands, etc.)

—+— NOTE: If the diverse parts of the body are brought together, —+— is placed in the spaces representing these parts

XX	compressing (describes such movements as lip pursing, nose crinkling, eye squinting or narrowing, furrowing of eyebrows, etc.)	⟩⟨	twitching (describes such movements as the eye twitch, lip twitch, etc.; any muscular twitch)
X	crossing	✳	uncrossing
∼	relaxing	□	tensing
∼□	relaxing then tensing as in the flexing of muscles	⟩⟩	wiggling or trembling
∨	widening	∧	narrowing
⌐⌐	seated in erect position with both feet on the ground	⟍	seated in slumped position with legs extended

Basic Movement Symbols

人 standing erect	⟨ standing with left portion of the body forward
⟩ standing with right portion of the body forward	⋀ walking

(The following symbols are generally used in conjunction with the basic movement symbols.)

◯ unexpected or sudden cessation of a movement in progress

∅ no movement; blank facial expression

⟋W̩⟍ very rapid movements

⟋M⟍ very slow movements

ⱳⱳⱳⱳⱳ slowing down

⋀⋁⋀⋁⋀ speeding up

◠ barely discernible, slight

◡ half, semi-

⟟ less than half

ℓ left

ℛ right

= following the basic movement symbols, this sign would indicate that the movement has established its related pose. For example, ·X indicates the movement of crossing, X=indicates that some part of the body is in a crossed position; ↑ indicates an upward movement of some part of the body; ↑= indicates the retention of that position; ⊢—indicates pushing; ⊢=indicates the holding of a pushing position or leaning.

Examples of Abbreviations to Describe Unique Movements

tip	on tip toes
limp	limping or dragging one foot
wink	the quick closing of one eye with the intention of communicating something to the viewer
rep	repetition of the same movement several times
one	one of two, i.e., one eye, one hand, one leg, etc.
both	two of two, i.e., two eyes, two hands, two legs, etc.
smile	smile without sound
smile $\vee$ =	wide smile, teeth visible, held for some time
smile $\bigcirc$	barely discernible smile
lip wipe	used when tongue visibly moistens the lips
fist	clenched hand
swallow	used when the act is unusually visible
run } skip }	while symbols might have been developed, it was felt that in the average school situation these would be used infrequently
thumb	indicates the thumb of the hand or the large toe of the foot
fore	indicates forefinger
middle	indicates middle finger

(The author is relying on the information of the single-sheet form and the common understanding of English abbreviations to achieve intersubjective descriptions.)

The glossary is an effort to develop a shorthand for describing body movements. To provide for every possible body movement, even if this were possible, would be self-defeating for learning the glossary would become too formidable a task. It is, therefore, very important that glossary users understand that they may have to make up a symbol or abbreviation for a movement they observe. They may also need to combine symbols to describe a body movement more accurately. The fixed form of the observation sheet contributes to the clarity by indicating which part of the body is being referred to and the sequence the movement follows. Some examples of the flexible use of the symbols follow:

$\sim$ mmm slowly relaxing (This may apply to any part of the body.)

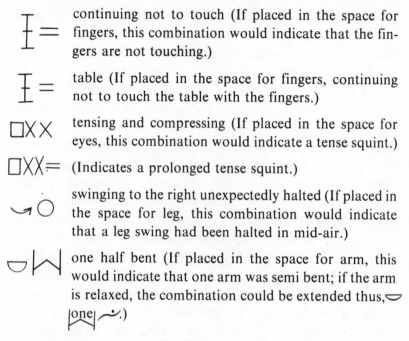

continuing not to touch (If placed in the space for fingers, this combination would indicate that the fingers are not touching.)

table (If placed in the space for fingers, continuing not to touch the table with the fingers.)

tensing and compressing (If placed in the space for eyes, this combination would indicate a tense squint.)

(Indicates a prolonged tense squint.)

swinging to the right unexpectedly halted (If placed in the space for leg, this combination would indicate that a leg swing had been halted in mid-air.)

one half bent (If placed in the space for arm, this would indicate that one arm was semi bent; if the arm is relaxed, the combination could be extended thus,⌣ |one| ⌣.)

The format of the nonverbal observation checklist to record body movements was crucial. The sheet has several functions: it must be able to indicate the verbal situation (as listed by Flanders) involved; it must help clarify and specify the movements represented by the basic movement symbols; it must provide a way of distinguishing the sequence of movements observed; it must provide for the reactions and ethnic backgrounds of the observers as well as of the observees.

The present checklist is a considerable modification of the first effort, which was used by the students of the graduate workshop that this author directed at the University of Illinois in 1971. The first effort tried to include spatial and touching relationships among people as well as all the parts of the body, but this was more than most observers could cope with. They tended to ignore the spatial relations column completely, generally expressing the opinion that the furniture in the classroom interfered with most of the normal changes in spatial relationships that might otherwise occur and with their ability to observe those changes that did occur. The description of touching behavior seemed to encounter similar difficulties. Furthermore, the quality of a touch is difficult to estimate from the back of a room.

An unexpected difference was found in the use of the form by middle-class white observers and middle-class black observers regarding the extensive listing of the different parts of the body. Since the lessons for using the forms were all given by this author and all the observers attended all sessions, it was reasonable to expect similarity among students in filling out the form. Instead the middle-class white observers tried to fill in every space provided for under parts of the body, an almost impossible feat given the imposed time limits. The blacks did what this author had assumed would be done; they described only those movements that seemed to be involved in communicating meaning. The significance of this difference may be linguistically based, but it certainly warrants investigation. It was, however, clear that not all parts of the body could be described by observers accurately—that observers needed to concentrate their efforts.

Only one Flanders situation was used per observation period. The observer recorded movements only when a student was responding to the teacher or only when the teacher was giving directions or during any other of Flanders' situations as decided prior to observation. Flanders' number system was used to indicate the particular classroom situation under study. The accompanying checklist is the most recent version of the single-sheet form; it will probably be modified in the future as experience is gained in its use.

The present form is very specific about the parts of the body contained in the head and upper torso. It is far less specific about the lower torso and this part of the form should be used only when movements in the lower torso are significant to the total body impression. This weighting of the form was decided because of the nature of most school settings. Students are generally behind furniture, either seated at their desks or, if standing, hidden from observers by furniture. Teachers have more mobility, but they, too, are predominantly seen as upper torsos and heads, the lower torso tucked behind desks and the heads of other students.

Recording the sequence of movements is aided by the six colums in each row of body parts. The placement of the glossary symbols is determined by the part of the body being described and the temporal position of the movement in the total sequence being described. If the hand and eyes move simultaneously, descriptions are placed in the same column; if the hand moves before the eyes do, then the description of the eyes is placed in the column following the one containing the description of the hand, i.e., hands in column 1, eyes in column 2.

Sequences of movements are described at the *initial portion of each* Flanders situation for a duration of 3 seconds. Research seems to indicate that the onset of an interaction or of any situation leaves its imprint on the entire occurrence. The time limit enables observers to enter into other aspects of the nonverbal observation checklist. After the 3-second description is completed, an observer immediately tries to record her or his own reactions to the nonverbal movements of the observee, ignoring, as much as possible, the verbal contents of the student-teacher interaction.

The third phase of the observation involves verification of the observer's impressions by listening to the content of the classroom talk. The ethnic background and the sex of the observer and the observee are recorded so that the reactions of diverse ethnic groups to, say, typical movements of black Americans may be surveyed and eventually analyzed. Each sequence of movements requires a separate form.

Several of my students worked in teams of two. One observed students of a particular ethnic background, the other observed the teacher responding to them. Others worked alone simply concentrating on the members of an ethnic group.

To obtain some idea of the reliability of the instrument, six observers, trained by the author in six two-hour sessions, were asked to describe the same individual during a class hour without communicating with each other. The Flanders' category for the experiment was #4, "Teacher asks questions;" it was used so that the teacher could involve the intended observee more frequently than might have otherwise been the case. In this instance the reliability of the glossary and of the temporal sequencing surpassed the .91 coefficient of reliability, that is, observers generally used the same sequence of movements and the same glossary symbols for the movements. However, only eight instances were described. The class was well behaved, and there were a few distractions or unpredictable moves. It is difficult to know from so little data whether this level of reliability would be obtained under more complicated or adverse conditions.

There was poor reliability for the impression and verification columns of the checklist. The observers, three blacks and three who described themselves as middle-class whites, seemed to split according to their background in recording their own impressions. The observee was a black male in the ninth grade. The black observers persistently circled the following adjectives: smart aleck, bored, careless, and desirous of attention. The three middle-class white observers persistently circled the following adjectives: confident, knowledgeable, defiant. Listening to what was actually said, that is, verifying original impressions, did not seem to change the original impressions.

Though this part of the checklist was not reliable regarding the observee, it proved to be an excellent vehicle for discussion among the six. For instance, one of the black observers asked the three whites, "Didn't you see the way he stood with one knee bent and the other side of his body jutting out? And then the way he would throw glances around the room. Why he was just saying, 'Look at me, I'm special,' and he wasn't meaning in school." The whites had noticed the movements, indeed, they had described them, but they had felt these reflected confidence. None of them thought the boy was being smart aleck, although during the last two questions he seemed to become defiant.

NONVERBAL OBSERVATION CHECKLIST

Ethnicity of observer ___ Set of observer ___

Ethnicity of observee ___ Sex of observee ___

Flanders Interaction Situation # ___

Parts of Body	Body Movement Sequence						Own impression of observee (Circle those that apply)	Verification
	1	2	3	4	5	6		What was said or what happened
Head							Relaxed	
Hair							Amused	
Forehead							Smart aleck	
Eyebrows							Enthused	
Eyes							Confident	
Nose							Knowledgeable	
Cheeks							Interested	
Lips/Mouth							Pensive	
Chin/Jaw							Comprehending	
Neck							Confused	
Shoulders							Bored	
Chest							Nervous	
Arms							Uncomfortable	
Elbows							Defiant	
Hands							Threatening	
Hips							Involved	
Legs							Careless	
Knees							Embarrassed	
Feet							Desirous of attention ___	
Whole body (Circle)	Walking Running Skipping Hopping Dancing Standing Sitting						Other:	
Other								

Unusual or significant classroom conditions

Conversations of this kind hold promise of increasing real understanding among teachers. Thus, despite the noted unreliability, these columns were retained. By comparing their impressions of body movements, teachers can learn from each other and increase their awareness of their own unsubstantiated interpretations.

In a survey of the observations of the thirty-two people who have used the checklist, observations were classified according to the ethnicity of the observee and the described body movements. Nineteen blacks, all males, were observed in typical classroom situations. The number of body movement descriptions was tallied to determine the ratio between total descriptions and the number of times a particular movement was made. Because of such difficulties as some observers filling in all the available spaces, while others limited their descriptions, the proportional analysis of body movements has not been validated, but some body movements were clearly more frequent than others. Among these were:

Holding the head high and tilted to one side with the chin jutting slightly outward

Laughing and seeming to mumble to oneself

Turning the body on one foot several times while conversing with others

Frequent movement away from and then closer to the group

Tapping out a rhythm with feet, hands, and head while doing a school task and with no music present

Frequent hair combing

Looking downward while talking to the teacher

Much "play" fighting with other males

Holding thumbs in pants pockets, hands hanging outside

While the observers' impressions of these movements were also recorded, there was no significant consistency between the impressions and the movements. Differences may be due to diverse ethnicities among the middle-class white group;

personality may also be a factor. Not enough observations have been made to come to any conclusion.

FOOTNOTES

[1]Ned A. Flanders, *Teacher Influence, Pupil Attitudes, and Achievement.* Minneapolis, University of Minnesota, U.S. Office of Education, Cooperative Research Project No. 397, 1960.

[2]Ray L. Birdwhistell, *Kinesics and Context* (Philadelphia: University of Pennsylvania Press, 1970) pp. 257-282.

[3]Ibid., p. 258.

[4]Ibid., p. 260.

[5]Ibid.

[6]Ibid.

Representing Ethnic Differences in Social Value Patterns

The possibility of visually picturing differences in the social value patterns of diverse ethnic groups led me to look for more succinct and possibly powerful ways of representing such differences. Initially, the three sets of descriptors yielded a straightforward visual image based on the six continuums (the nature of valuing was not included) somewhat as follows:

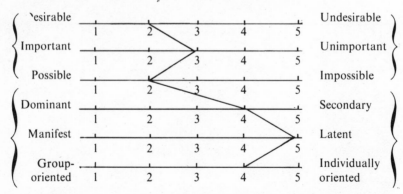

Such a visual image allowed differences that might exist between two ethnic groups to be summarized by comparing simplified representations, i.e., the line joining points is a simplification of the six continuums. What was lost and perhaps misrepresented by this device was the different influences each descriptor might have as well as variations in influence that might occur under different social value patterns. It was reasoned, however, that since the differences between groups was being sought, the actual nature of the interaction between the continuums need not be known if it were assumed that the nature of the interactions were the same or similar from group to group. In other words, "desirable," "important," and the other descriptors were considered to relate to each other in a similar way regardless of ethnic group. This assumption would make the interaction of the twelve descriptors a universal of humanness having the same stability as such characteristics as the human hand.

With this reservation in mind, the sets of descriptors can be arranged in a 3 x 3 matrix without indicating any significance for their interaction:

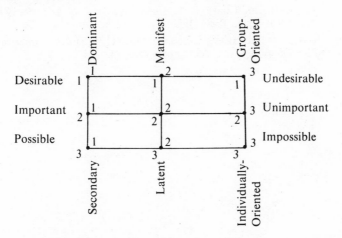

This matrix format (which would be derived from the median of responses to appropriate questions, as described in Chapter VII) allows a social value pattern to be described by a series of numbers. It also allows for the subtraction and addition of matrixes, so that a numerical representation of differences between groups can be developed and even a representation of a social value pattern's strength within a group.

At present, this work has not been developed any further. The intention is to explore scaling techniques that might be applicable. It has been suggested that the method of equal-appearing intervals, first described by Thurstone and Chave,[1] might be useful in obtaining a quantitative model. Multivariate analysis of ordinal data as carried out by Jae-On Kim[2] has also been suggested as a possibility.

Whether a numerical representation proves feasible or the linear representation is retained, the basic question for future research is whether any correlation exists between the "pictured" difference in social value patterns and observable conflicts and/or compatibilities arising among diverse ethnic groups.

FOOTNOTES

[1]Thurstone, L. L., and Chave, E. J., *The Measurement of Attitudes* (Chicago: University of Chicago Press, 1929).

[2]Kim, Jae-On, "Multivariate Analysis of Ordinal Variables," *American Journal of Sociology,* Vol. 81, September, 1975, pp. 261-298.